MW01712593

"*To The Church of This Generation, Write* is an urgent message for the church in this day. Rachel Quirt has shared graciously and compassionately from her heart and from the heart of God the need for the church to wake up and respond to the Word of the Lord. She highlights the deception of the enemy regarding sexual immorality and calls us to repent and turn back to the place of precious purity. Rachel brings clarity and depth to many sensitive issues and expounds upon the love and mercy of a Heavenly Father who desperately wants His people to walk in His best. This book brings awareness to many issues in our culture, but most importantly, it calls us to act! It calls us to radically examine and change how we live our lives. Rachel's transparency and honesty is so refreshing and allows us to connect with the heart of God for each of our lives! We highly recommend this book, knowing that it is a prophetic call to the Body of Christ to free itself from the chains of the world and fall in love with Jesus all over again!"

Cameron & Sandra Jeffs,
Lead Pastors
Impact Church,
Kingston, Ontario

To The Church of This Generation, Write:

'A Call to Repentance & Purity'

Rachel Quirt

TO THE CHURCH OF THIS GENERATION, WRITE

ISBN: 978-1-77069-792-8

Word Alive Press
131 Cordite Road, Winnipeg, MB R3W 1S1
www.wordalivepress.ca

WORD ALIVE PRESS
Just Write!

Cataloguing in Publication information may be obtained from Library and Archives Canada.

I dedicate this book...

To all the exploited, everywhere, who struggle to be seen
and valued, and to have a voice that is heard.
I value you and I hear you.
It is an honour to speak on your behalf.

To my mother and late father. You prayed for your family so
diligently all these years...you are loved!

TABLE OF CONTENTS

ACKNOWLEDGMENTS ix
FOREWORD xiii
INTRODUCTION xv
PREFACE xxi

SECTION ONE: JUDGMENT

one THE ETERNAL PURPOSES OF GOD:
A Panoramic View 3

two INTIMACY WITH THE KING:
For Such a Time as This 11

three CASTING OFF RESTRAINTS:
Falling Asleep in the Lap of Sexual Immorality 19

four INNOCENCE COMPROMISED:
Consequence of Sexual Immorality 29

SECTION TWO: RESTORATION

five REFINER'S FIRE:
The Kiln of God's Glory 49

six THE PRESENCE OF JESUS:
The Indwelling Glory 59

CONCLUSION 69

ACKNOWLEDGMENTS

My deepest gratitude to…

Spiritual leaders throughout my Christian walk: Pastor Bob and Candy Boutillier, Pastor Shawn and Pastor Mary Bowers, Pastor Colin and Sharen Cleugh, and Pastor Cameron and Pastor Sandra Jeffs. Thank you for so diligently proclaiming the Word of God in truth and love, and for giving me a great foundation in the gospel of Jesus Christ. Thank you for your discipleship and mentoring, and for giving me an opportunity to grow in my trust and faith through practically applying the Word of God in my circle of influence.

The women of Calvary Pentecostal Church in Gananoque, Ontario: thank you for walking with me through wilderness moments and for giving me a safe place to heal from the wounds of the world. Thank you for the eleven years of opportunity to lead and grow in teaching and proclaiming the Word of God. Thank you for believing that there was potential and an anointing upon my life to help fulfill the purposes of God in my generation.

Sandy Buchanan, who helped behind the scenes in many ways, like giving me her Bible when I didn't have one as a new Christian. You gave me a hug when I really didn't want one, but needed it, and walked up to me at a Bible study and said, "Call me, I think I need to share a personal story with you." And the rest is history as well as friendship. Love you.

Heather O'Reilly…God has uniquely shaped our friendship in ways I didn't know could exist. There has been tremendous blessing upon all of our three-hour or more discussions. Who knew we had that much information in us. Thank you for the day you decided to stay longer and to let me into your heart, as it is my heart that has been changed forever by your friendship. Love you.

Impact Church, what can I say…you have all been so unbelievably the body of Christ from the moment I walked in the doors on February 29, 2012, as a full-time member. What I have experienced in the year I have been part of Impact assembly has been what I call Spirit of Adoption. I can't express the overwhelming flow of love poured out upon my family and me. I look forward to what our Heavenly Father has in store for His church in the coming years!

My precious family, thank you for believing I could begin walking out what has been germinating in my heart for almost a decade. Thank you, Brianna, for dragging me to the gym in the midst of writing this book, as it always gave me perspective. Thank you, Richard, for listening and participating in conversations that were tough because of the subject: sex trafficking and all it entails. Thank you for your supportive words and actions, as I took time off work to write and to start Arise & Shine Ministries. Thank you most of all, my precious, chosen husband, for your tremendous integrity to your family. There are things nobody sees but your Heavenly Father and me… they don't go unnoticed by Him or me. You are, outside of Jesus, my closest friend. I love you and am so grateful that you are my husband.

Jesus—without you I would have perished fifteen years ago. You truly lifted me out of the miry clay and set my feet upon a rock. May we diligently be a light and a messenger unto the world, as you desired!

> *May the God who gives endurance and encouragement give you a spirit of unity among yourselves as you follow Christ Jesus, so that with one heart and mouth you may glorify the God and Father of our Lord Jesus Christ.* (Romans 15:5–6)

FOREWORD

It is with great delight that I write this foreword for my friend Rachel Quirt. The following words will reveal the love and respect Sharen (my wife) and I have for her.

We first met Rachel in 2004 when we moved to Gananoque, Ontario, to pastor Calvary Pentecostal Church. Rachel was not only a committed member of the congregation but a leader of the women's ministry as well.

It was quickly obvious to both Sharen and me that Rachel was very sensitive to the things of God and uncommonly mature (being a fairly new Christian at the time). What was not apparent to us that day was the deep friendship that would be formed in our lives and how much we would come to rely on her as prayerful supporter and encourager.

The reasons for this wonderful relationship are the following:

First, Rachel has a teachable spirit. In order to be teachable you have to have an open mind and heart. I have observed her openness to learn, grow and change as God works in her life. She not only is emotionally impacted by God's Word upon hearing it, but does the hard work to actually bringing her behaviour in line with God's will and plan.

Second, Rachel is very sensitive to the voice of God. She not only knows the voice of the Spirit but she purposefully puts it into practice in her own life.

Third, Rachel is a great mentor to those around her. Because other women respect her authenticity, she is sought out by others for her wise advice and counsel.

As you read, you are about to hear the voice of the Great Shepherd earnestly pleading with his church much as He did as He overlooked Jerusalem (Matthew 23:37) just prior to His trial, crucifixion, death and resurrection.

To The Church of This Generation, Write is a wake-up call and a must read for any Christ-follower concerned with the effects of the way we live on both this generation and the ones to follow.

The sexualization of our society is obvious to any truth observer of our culture. What is not obvious or common is the question, will you be honest and respond intentionally, or—like we often do in church—say, "Wow, that was a great service/message," and leave and never do a thing about it?

Prepare to be challenged to a deeper personal commitment in your relationship to God and others.

Colin Cleugh
Lead Pastor
The Cornerstone
Gananoque, Ontario

INTRODUCTION

"The truth isn't sexy."[1] The human trafficking crisis is an estimated $32 billion industry, globally. It is quickly becoming the largest crime trade in the world. Canada has become a port, source, and destination country for sex traffickers and perpetrators. Sex traffickers are reportedly earning up to $280,000 a year from each trafficked person—usually women and girls, because tragically, they are exploited over and over again. In Ontario, Canada, pimps are purchasing teenage girls for approximately $5,000.[2]

I can't think of anything darker than the sex-trafficking crisis, except perhaps our silence—and, in some cases permission, promotion, and participation. The Christian majority is not involved directly with human trafficking, but are we involved in the sexualization and objectification of women and children? Are we involved with its promotion, which leads to the extreme end of sexualization—human trafficking?

Originally, I was writing this book to the secular community, to bring awareness and action to the issue of sexualization and objectification of

---

[1] Term used from the Salvation Army website, Vancouver, Canada.

[2] http:www.havocscope.com/number-of-human-trafficking-victims-in-canada, accessed March 27, 2013

women and children in the media, and its impact on this and future generations. I wanted to encourage and enhance an understanding and awareness that the overt sexualizing and objectifying of women and children in our culture cannot be disconnected from the issue of the sex-trafficking crisis. We cannot overlook that we are potentially, mentally sexually abusing every boy and girl in the next generation through the onslaught and acceptability of soft pornography in all forms of the media, which even our youngest children are exposed to daily without our explicit consent, at malls, on billboards and on magazines at the checkout, in movies—everywhere.

I was about one third of the way through writing when my target audience changed. It changed after a brief conversation with a Pastor, who said, "If I could just say this to you: don't neglect to bring this message to the church." These few words were a catalyst to moments with God, and wrestling in my spirit over the direction God was asking me to take. In a few short months I decided through many confirmations from God that I would write, first, to the church.

> *And the Lord said to Samuel: "See, I am about to do something in Israel that will make the ears of everyone who hears of it tingle. At that time I will carry out against Eli everything I spoke against his family—from beginning to end. For I told him that I would judge his family forever because of the* <u>*sin he knew about;*</u> *his sons made themselves contemptible, and he* <u>*failed to restrain them.*</u>*"* (1 Samuel 3:11–13)

Silence concerning sin we know about is never acceptable for leaders of God's people, nor is it acceptable for God's people to be silent toward society. We are to be an example and a light unto the world. We not only have a message to proclaim, we are to be the representation of that message. I am confused that we seem to think we can eradicate human trafficking in our world when the church and society is itself engaged in sexual immorality. Humanity is in dire straits, and it needs the message of the gospel. However, the church is unable to deliver that message with boldness and authority because we are practicing the same things as the world. The enemy is conquering God's people, right now, on the battlefield of sexual immorality. I've heard it said that warfare is when both sides want the same territory. The enemy, through sexual immorality, is stripping us of our favour with God and man, and he is covering us with shame. However, God is calling His people to a place of repentance and purity. Repentance brings deliverance and a refreshing from Christ, and purity brings the glory of God—His presence! It is only His presence that separates us from the nations of the world.

This book is a prophetic call to the church to return to God in purity and righteousness, as well as a prophetic observation that the enemy is dedicated to stripping us of God's glory so that the Israelite nation will not receive a revelation of their Messiah and be saved! The Apostle Paul speaks clearly that we, the church, are to bring the Jewish people to a place of envy through recognition of the glory of God in and upon our lives. How can we perform this function if we are stripped of glory and filled with shame through our compromise with sexual immorality?

John Maxwell says, "A leader is one who knows the way, goes the way, and shows the way." Jesus is the leader of the church and He is the Way. He has told us the way, He has gone the way, and He has shown the way—as disciples, should we not follow? *"When a man believes in me, he does not believe in me only, but in the one who sent me. When he looks at me, he sees the one who sent me. I have come into the world as a light, so that no one who believes in me should stay in darkness"* (John 12:44–46). We need not stay in darkness to the enemy's tactics of sexual immorality. We have everything to win this battle: the appropriation of the blood of Jesus Christ brought about by repentance. The church is called to represent Jesus on earth. When people look at us, should they not see Jesus and the Father, just as Jesus said, *"When he looks at me, he sees the one who sent me"* (John 12:45)? Do the world and the Jewish nation see the one who sent us?

In hopes of allowing the Holy Spirit room to speak directly to you through His word, and to let His Spirit break upon your heart in ways He desires to bring change, if any is required, I have kept personal thoughts and opinions to a minimum, except in Chapter Four. I also hope you will be greatly encouraged, as a lover of Jesus, that He is on the move across the nations, and I trust that this message, through the witness of the Holy Spirit, will burn in our hearts, bringing forth His eternal purposes.

WARNINGS

Warnings are only effective in their proper season. For example, my fifteen-year-old daughter is dragging—yes, dragging—me to the gym three times a week to work out with her. I noticed the other day, as we were entering the front doors, that although it's the beginning of summer, there's a sign posted above the door that reads:

WARNING: Watch for falling snow or ice!

This is a good warning…when it's winter. During the summer, it can be safely ignored because although the warning sign is up, it holds no weight or bearing on us. You would be hard-pressed to find anyone who would take it seriously. However, the winter season will come, and suddenly it will be wise for everyone to pay attention to that particular warning of falling snow or ice.

Unlike my gym, which leaves up useless warnings out of season, our Heavenly Father gives us warnings at the proper time when we might heed His instructions and benefit from them with blessings, protection, and safety. In light of this, let God give us ears to hear, eyes to see and a heart to perceive all He is saying, and doing, in *our generation*.

> *See to it that you do not refuse him who speaks. If they (Israel) did not escape when they refused him who <u>warned</u> them on the earth, how much less will we, if we turn away from him who <u>warns</u> us from heaven? At that time his voice shook the earth, but now he has promised (and God is not a man, that he can lie), "Once more I will shake not only the earth but also the heavens." The words "once more" indicate the removing of what can be shaken—that is, created things—so that what cannot be shaken may remain.*

Therefore, since we are receiving a kingdom that cannot be shaken, let us be thankful, and so worship God acceptably with reverence and awe, for our "God is a consuming fire." (Hebrews 12:25–29, emphasis added)

PREFACE

"For it is time for judgment to begin with the family of God"
(1 Peter 4:17)

Throughout biblical history, when God was about to bring judgment or restoration upon His people, He first sent a forerunner or prophet to proclaim His message to the people, and the corresponding desired response. Because of God's love and justice, He sent His prophets often to the people of Israel, giving them fair warning of pending judgment, that they might repent of their sins and turn back to God with all of their hearts (Jeremiah 7:25). If they rejected God's prophet, and the prophet's message, then God, after a season, allowed judgment to overtake His people. In the midst of judgment, God still sent His prophets to call His people back to Him, if they would but repent and turn from their wickedness. God's heart is never to bring judgment on His people, but if they choose to engage in sin, He must, in His righteousness and justice, bring correction and discipline. His presence cannot dwell with sin, which hinders the flow of relationship between God and His covenant people, thwarting His eternal purposes and plans in the world.

The chosen people of God—historical Israel, and now the church—have always carried a *corporate* prophetic call. It is their duty on earth to be a prophetic voice to the nations. This prophetic role is to be *a spokesperson for God*, releasing His message to the nations, of repentance and salvation through Jesus Christ for all who would choose to receive Him. This is the mandate of the church, God's people: a ministry of reconciliation. This prophetic call, to be *a voice to the nations*, holds immense responsibility. We are to consistently seek to be in unity and peace with one another and, in a deeply intimate walk with Christ, freed from sin, clearly hear God's heart, mind, and message, releasing it to the nations—bringing forth the kingdom of God on earth as it is in heaven. The purpose of this *corporate* prophetic voice is to *proclaim the message of salvation to the nations*, until the fullness of the Gentiles comes into the kingdom of God. This is so we might bring the remnant of the Jewish nation, reserved for salvation, a revelation of Jesus, their Messiah. This is a great mandate and call upon the Gentile church of Jesus Christ. The apostle Paul understood this mandate and laboured tirelessly among the Gentiles in hopes of bringing salvation to his Jewish brothers. The church now carries this mandate, and is to diligently labour toward individual and corporate intimacy with Jesus, that we might be filled with His glory, bringing in the fullness of the Gentiles, causing the Jewish remnant envy unto salvation, as the apostle Paul desired.

However, it seems that the present Gentile church has lost, misunderstood, or never known this prophetic vision. We understand the mandate to go into all the world, making disciples, baptizing them and teaching them to obey everything Jesus commanded, but we have lost the panoramic view of God's eternal prophetic vision. A vision of a fullness of Gentiles in the kingdom of God, so intimate with Jesus and clothed in His glory that they would cause a disobedient, blinded Jewish nation to be moved to envy. The church must have this panoramic prophetic vision restored. We must understand the need to press into the high calling of getting to know Jesus more. We want to know Jesus more just for the sake of a love relationship with Him; however, we also need to know what is at stake if we do not press in. We must receive revelation of a profound need to be freed from sin and filled with His glory, advancing the kingdom of God until the fullness of Gentiles is brought to salvation and intimacy with Jesus. We cannot give the Jewish people what we do not have ourselves!

God calls the church to be a prophetic voice and a conscience to the nations, but we have lost that prophetic voice through sin. God desires to *wake up* the *conscience* of the church that we might be able to, once again, bring His prophetic voice to the nations and awaken their conscience. In this book, I speak of a particular sin God seeks to root out of His people. He wants to root it out that He might not bring judgment, but instead bring intimacy and His glory to dwell within individuals and, corporately, within the Gentile church. This sin is sexual immorality. Sexual immorality, in all its variants, is running rampant in His church. Instead of being filled with intimacy and God's glory, we are filled with shame and distanced from God! We have become blinded, weak, and vulnerable to the oppression of the enemy. Weighted down and hindered from fulfilling the ultimate mandate and eternal purpose of God in this world. I believe God is calling for repentance and a return to His holiness that we might once again see His face in intimacy, and be filled with His glory!

JUDGMENT TO BEGIN IN THE HOUSE OF GOD

Many of us recoil when we hear the word judgment, especially when it's used in the church. We have an unpleasant taste in our mouths, perhaps from some experiences with legalism, traditions, and fire-and-brimstone preaching. Sometimes when we hear the word judgment, we think condemnation and no grace. But that's not the judgment I'm speaking of, nor is it the judgment God is speaking of when He says, *"For it is time for judgment to begin with the family of God"* (1 Peter 4:17).

It's my understanding that there are two types of biblical judgment. There's the judgment we know of as the wrath of God. The wrath of God occurs when the conviction of the Holy Spirit is refused repeatedly, until the heart is so seared that it can no longer be brought to repentance and is hardened to the things of God. When a person rejects God and His conviction, eventually the presence of God lifts off of that person and, because He no longer protects them, the enemy gains full access and judgment comes (John 3:36; Romans 1:18, 24). This kind of judgment seems to arise first in people's minds. Then there's the judgment at the heart of this book—the judgment God brings to refine His people, freeing them from bondage to sin, setting the captives free, purifying their hearts that they may live in intimacy with Jesus, filled with His glory.

In the prophet Malachi's day, the Jews were in a state of casting off restraints and engaging in sinful behaviours. They no longer believed God was going to bring about the promises of the prophets—promises of Israel being a significant people and God coming to His temple with revival, arriving in His majesty and power to exalt His kingdom in the sight of the surrounding nations. Through unbelief, they began to doubt God's love for them, and His justice. Since He had not come in judgment to exalt His people among the nations, the Jews began to stop taking His laws seriously. Feeling justified in their sins because of God's seeming lack of presence and response, they brought multiple accusations against Him, which the prophet Malachi addressed. Throughout the book of Malachi, we read about God saying through His prophet, "I have said to you…But you ask, how have we…?" Constantly they justified their sins by saying, how have we shown contempt for your name? How have we defiled you? How have we robbed you? How…how…how? Malachi tells us that they wearied God with their words by saying, "*All who do evil are good in the eyes of the LORD, and he is pleased with them*" or "*Where is the God of justice?*" (Malachi 2:17)[3]

Is this not what we do in our hearts, as well? Have we accused God because He seems to have delayed His coming to His people with revival, or seems to have delayed fulfilling His promises to us? And because He is seemingly not tangibly involved in our lives, have we begun to no longer take His requirements for righteous living seriously? Have we lost the prophetic vision, and now justify our sins with God's seeming

---

[3] Introduction to Malachi, NIV, 2000, p. 1416,1417, *Reflecting God Study Bible*, Zondervan Publishing House, Grand Rapids, MI 49530, USA.
Commentaries influencing my understanding of the book of Malachi: Matthew Henry's Commentary
http://www.christnotes.org/commentary.php?com=mhc&b=39&c=0

absence? Casting off restraints, have we allowed sexual immorality inside our walls of salvation? God's word says there must not be even a hint of sexual immorality among the church, as this is not appropriate for God's people (Ephesians 5:3). In this context, the apostle Paul gave the newly converted Gentiles warning to be particularly aware and conscious of this type of behaviour, because they were coming out of a culture that did not believe or think sexual immorality was wrong. Paul was trying to warn the believers to not allow even a hint of sexual immorality in their lives so it could not find a place from which it could continue to grow. Sensual lusts have a way of never being sufficiently gratified, and thus continue to want to be fed until they grow into something that places the believer in danger of losing out on the kingdom of God (1 Corinthians 6:9).

In Malachi, God did answer His people's charges, but He answered them by stating that the Lord they were seeking to come and judge the nations would come, but He would *first* come and judge His people. He would first come and purify His own people before He judged the surrounding nations. God says, *"So I will come near to you for judgment. I will be quick to testify against..."* (Malachi 3:1–5).

Why does God judge the church first? As I've explained, Israel, and now the church, has always had a calling to be a *corporate*, *prophetic voice* and *conscience* to the nations. This means we need to be able to stand in God's intimate council, hear His voice, receive His message, and proclaim it with authority and boldness to the nations, causing their consciences to be seared, and possibly turn them to repent of their wickedness. However, we have lost our intimacy with Jesus, and thus our prophetic voice is silenced and the nations scoff at us because we engage in the precise things we are speaking to them about. As we read in 1 Corinthians 6:2–3, *"...Do you not know that the Lord's people will judge the world? ...Do you not know that we will judge angels? How much more the things of this life!"* The apostle Paul goes on to say that it's to our shame that we, God's people, are unable to judge even between ourselves, because we engage in the very same behaviours. It is God's desire to *first wake up the conscience of the church,* that we might be able to bring His voice to the surrounding nations. He awakens our conscience by first bringing judgment like a refiner's fire—a fire that burns up all the dross, and refines and purifies like gold or silver (Malachi 3:4).

God's answer to Israel in Malachi's day was 1) *He will come*, 2) He will *draw near*, 3) He will draw near *for judgment*, and 4) will be *quick to testify against sin* in His people's lives, and purge everything that is not of Him.

This past Easter Monday, the Holy Spirit spoke these words to me:

> *God is not coming to bring judgment on His people, He is coming to bring judgment on the enemy's activity (sin) in people's lives. However, if His people choose to hold on to their sin, then judgment will come upon them as well.*

John Bevere describes judgment this way: "It is a decision for or against." He also cautions, "Judgment delayed, does not mean judgment denied." When the Holy Spirit convicts a person of sin, He is giving opportunity for that individual to receive His grace, mercy, and empowerment to receive freedom from the captivity of sin, if they will repent. However, if that person chooses to disregard the conviction in their heart, God's presence will lift and that person will have to deal with the consequences of their sin, and will not receive grace.

May we have humble and contrite hearts that we would choose to let go of any sins of which the Holy Spirit convicts us. May we not think that God does not see us, or does not care. And may we not, through loss of prophetic vision, cast off restraint and engage in sinful lusts of the flesh.

> *Prayer:*
> *Heavenly Father, you see your precious son or daughter before you, and conviction has fallen upon them even now, so I ask that through your Holy Spirit you would come to them wherever they are, and as they humble their heart before you, and repent of their sin of sexual immorality, I ask that you would root out and tear down the oppression of the enemy that has kept them in shackles and in darkness. Father, I pray that your glory would arise upon them and*

push back the darkness and the lies of the enemy, exposing any area where he has been secretly active in the life of your child. I speak and declare freedom over their lives, and a release from the heavy burden of carrying their, perhaps secret, sin. I release the precious blood of Jesus Christ over your child to cover and wash away all of their sin, and to wash away all of the darkness and pain that it has caused. Let their mind, heart, and spirit be free, in Jesus' Name! Let life be restored, and forgiveness released into their lives, bringing a refreshing from Jesus and a fresh revelation of the amazing grace of their God! In Jesus' mighty Name. Amen!
Be set free, son/daughter of God!

SECTION ONE

judgment

one

THE ETERNAL PURPOSES OF GOD: A Panoramic View

> *You will arise and have compassion on Zion, for it is time to show favour to her; the appointed time has come. For her stones are dear to your servants; her very dust moves them to pity.* (Psalm 102:13–14)

In the last few years, I've enjoyed dabbling in painting. While painting, there are times when I am in very close proximity to the piece in order to paint particular details, such as highlights in a beard or on a piece of clothing. These details are crucial to the overall effect. However, I also must frequently step back and peruse the canvas from a distance to consider whether I've used the right colour, shade, or highlight. Have I placed the paint in the right spot, or used enough paint to capture that which I intended? Then there are times when I need to stand at an even greater distance and view the painting from across the room, ensuring I am presenting the overall intended effect. I call this action a panoramic view—an unbroken, sweeping, and comprehensive vision of my work. This action aids in reminding me of my ultimate goal, and provides me with a greater recognition of where I need to place my next brushstroke.

Like this panoramic view of a painting, God desires the church to take a few steps back from all of the detailed work of ministry in order to capture the overall effect and purpose of our salvation. It would be wise of us to take a moment to observe one's salvation from a distance, and perceive the bigger eternal purposes of God's saving and delivering work in the world. Often, we read portions of scripture and, although we have a reasonable understanding of them, unconsciously set them aside as being for *another* generation, not our own. For example, have you ever read the book of Romans and skipped right over all of the times the apostle Paul speaks of his desire for his Jewish brothers to be saved through the *envy* of the Gentile church? Romans 10:1 says, *"Brothers, my heart's desire and prayer to God for the Israelites is that they may be saved."* And Romans 11:11b states, *"Again I ask: Did they stumble so as to fall beyond recovery? Not at all! Rather, because of their transgression, salvation has come to the Gentiles to make Israel envious."*

God desires to let us know that the time for entering into all His fullness of glory and life, bringing envy to the Jewish nation that they might be saved, *is here!* We are a chosen generation, a chosen vessel, a chosen people, to see Christ return, and dwell amongst His people in all of His glory and splendour, ushering in the harvest of end-time souls—the fullness of the Gentiles. A chosen people to be so intimate with Jesus that the Jewish nation is brought to envy, receiving a revelation of their Messiah, Jesus. The Gentile church has come into their royal position, adopted as God's children, betrothed of Christ, for such a time as this.

Zechariah 12:10 states,

> *And I will pour out on the house of David and the inhabitants of Jerusalem a spirit of grace and supplication. They will look on me, the one they have pierced, and they will mourn for him as one mourns for an only child, and grieve bitterly for him as one grieves for a firstborn son.*

Clark's commentary on this scripture[4] says,

> A *spirit of grace* will be God showing the Jews that he yet bears favour to them and they shall be aroused to *fervent and continual prayer* for the restoration of God's divine favour. Christ will be preached to them; and they shall look upon and believe in him whom they pierced, and crucified at Jerusalem. This shall then produce *deep and sincere repentance; a bitterness of soul*, to think they crucified the Lord of life and glory, and continued to blaspheme him, since that time. (Emphasis added)

On March 4, 2004, at a *Show Me Your Glory* conference in Toronto, Ontario, during worship, I received a picture in my mind's eye of a long stream of people in light-blue prisoner uniforms with something white atop their heads, walking on a winding, dusty road. The road, and the multitudes of people, snaked into the distance until I could not see them anymore. The prisoners were walking in rows, close together, shoulder to shoulder. They had been freed and were travelling back home. As I was watching this, I saw in my spirit the word *EXILES* over their heads and I suddenly realized these people were Jewish exiles returning home. The white caps were Kippas, the Jewish cap.

Two days later, during morning intercession for the conference, I heard a lady share a vision of a rugged traveller carrying a perfectly balanced wooden bar across his shoulders, on each end was a chain holding a pail. One pail was filled with bread and the other pail, filled with water. She shared that she felt God was saying that the conference attendees were going to bring back to their communities what they received at the conference. I did not hear the rest of her sharing, because I was suddenly seeing a vision of Jesus as the traveller, and He was returning to His community, His hometown, Jerusalem. He was bringing the Bread of Life, and the Living Water—Jesus their Messiah, and the Holy Spirit, in order to feed the Jewish nation.

---

[4] *Commentary on the Bible*, by Adam Clarke [1831]. http://clarke.biblecommenter.com/zechariah/12.htm

At this time, the lady began to pray in her vision and at one point prayed for prisoners to either *return* or *come home* (I cannot remember which). As she spoke this, I began to weep uncontrollably—deep, heart-wrenching sobs. The Holy Spirit began to bring to mind the vision of the exiles I had seen two days prior. I then saw the exiles, still in their prisoner uniforms, wearing Kippas, kneeling in the same direction. I experienced this vision from the perspective of standing behind them. They were all kneeling as if in repentance, prayer, and worship. They were all facing something…I then felt the Holy Spirit impress these words on my heart: *"Once again, they will come, and turn toward My Holy Mountain, and worship Me in spirit, and in truth."*

Isaiah 27:13 says, *"And in that day a great trumpet will sound. Those who were perishing in Assyria and those who were exiled in Egypt will come and worship the LORD on the holy mountain in Jerusalem."* And Jeremiah 31:9 says, *"They will come with weeping; they will pray as I bring them back."*

The Bible also describes the Mountain of the LORD in the last days:

> *The mountain of the LORD's temple will be established as chief among the mountains; it will be raised above the hills, and all the nations will stream to it. Many peoples will come and say, "Come, let us go up to the mountain of the LORD, to the house of the God of Jacob. He will teach us his ways, so that we may walk in his paths." The law will go out from Zion, the word of the LORD from Jerusalem.* (Isaiah 2:2–3)

It's time for the corporate church to take a step back from all that we have been working toward and receive a panoramic view of God's eternal purposes for the church. If we don't understand or perceive the desired goal, we miss out on running our race effectively. We may even miss out on being in the right race. For example, how many Christians are running the race for themselves—for increased skills and talents, personal ministry, to be successful in this world, and so on—instead of running the race to know Christ more and see His purposes and plans worked out on earth? Although these are part of walking in relationship with Jesus, they are not the goal. The goal of the race is to individually and corporately, as the church around the nations, enter into a deep, personal, intimate relationship with Jesus, living in holiness that God may dwell within in His temple in all of His glory, bringing in the fullness of the Gentiles to salvation so that Israel can be brought to envy and be saved!

The apostle Paul understood this panoramic view of the eternal purposes of God. He states, in Romans 10:1, *"Brothers, my heart's desire and prayer to God for the Israelites is that they may be saved."* He goes on to say in Romans 9:2–4a, *"I have great sorrow and unceasing anguish in my heart. For I could wish that I myself were cursed and cut off from Christ for the sake of my brothers, those of my own race, the people of Israel."*

How the apostle Paul's heart must have broken over his past lack of understanding of God's eternal purposes in the world, as he remembered his former life, prior to meeting Christ. The apostle Paul, formerly the very zealous, but lacking in knowledge, Saul of Tarsus, persecuted and murdered Christians in hopes of preventing the spread of the gospel they preached. Now, after having met Jesus on the road to Damascus, and having received revelations from God about the mystery of the church, Paul is so *unceasingly anguished* and *sorrowful* in heart for Israel *to be saved*, that he would consider, if that would help, to be *cut off from Christ for their salvation!* Paul's heart, burdened with the salvation of his people, was willing to go to hell in their stead! Thankfully, by Jesus' death on the cross and His atonement this would never be a requirement, however, it shows how deeply burdened Paul was for the salvation of the Jewish people. I believe he understood deeply God's heart for His chosen people Israel, whom He calls the apple of His eye.

The apostle Paul revealed God's heart, highlighted in Jeremiah 31:20: *"Is not Ephraim my dear son, the child in whom I delight? Though I often speak against him, I still remember him. Therefore my heart yearns for him; I have great compassion for him, declares the LORD."*

This scripture reveals the heart of our Heavenly Father toward Israel, His firstborn, the apple of His eye. We see it spelled out again in the New Testament when we read about the Prodigal Son in Luke 15:11–24. I am going to quote the scripture almost in its entirety so that the poignancy of the story doesn't become lost, as you will see that it is a representation of our Heavenly Father's heart toward His firstborn, Israel.

> *There was a man who had two sons. The younger one said to his father, "Father, give me my share of the estate." So he divided his property between them.*
> *Not long after that, the younger son got together all he had, set off for a distant country and there squandered his wealth in wild living. After he had spent everything, there was a severe famine in that whole country, and he began to be in need. So he went and hired himself out to a citizen of that country, who sent him to his fields to feed pigs. He longed to fill his stomach with the pods that the pigs were eating, but no one gave him anything.*
> *When he came to his senses, he said, "How many of my father's hired men have food to spare, and here I am starving to death! I will set out and go back to my father and say to him: Father, I have sinned against heaven and against you. I am no longer worthy to be called your son; make me like one of your hired men." So he got up and went to his father.*
> *But while he was still a long way off, his father saw him and was filled with compassion for him; he ran to his son, threw his arms around him and kissed him.*
> *The son said to him, "Father, I have sinned against heaven and against you. I am no longer worthy to be called your son."*
> *But the father said to his servants, "Quick! Bring the best robe and put it on him. Put a ring on his finger and sandals on his feet. Bring the fattened calf and kill it. Let's have a feast and celebrate. For this son of mine was dead and is alive again; he was lost and is found." So they began to celebrate.*

Many of us can relate to and understand this story, as the majority of us have loved ones, whether it is a child or some other loved one, whom we desperately want to see returned to Jesus. We can relate to God's words: "*...although I have often spoken against him, I still remember him*" (Jeremiah 31:20).

On a personal note, I, without thinking about my choices, decided to leave home when I was sixteen. As with any home, there were certain things that I did not enjoy about my family life, but my leaving had nothing to do with my parents or family; it was a random thought that came into my head, and I acted on it. I recall conversing with a friend at school about the possibility of starting our grade eleven year at a school in a surrounding city. I picked this idea up and ran with it; she, however, stayed where she was. (This was wisdom; mine was not!) During this time, I am sure that my parents often spoke against me—my decisions—but they still yearned for me to come to my senses and come home!

This is also God's heart for the nation Israel, the Jewish people, His firstborn. His Fatherly heart yearns for them to see their plight of being blind, naked, wretched, and poor, that they might repent, turn and receive their salvation! His plan to bring this about rests upon the Gentile church fulfilling their calling and mandate to spread the gospel around the nations, bringing in the fullness of the Gentiles. Discipling them into a deep, intimate relationship with Jesus, helping them to become filled with His glory, causing Israel envy that they might see and receive their long-awaited Messiah!

Are we now catching a glimpse of the panoramic view of God's eternal purposes? Are we able to step back and see the call and mandate upon the Gentile church, so we can move forward with more focus and greater understanding of the need for an intimate relationship with Jesus, and a desire to be filled with His glory? Having stepped back to a greater distance from the picture, can we see where we need to place our efforts?

two

INTIMACY WITH THE KING:
For Such a Time as This

"*...And who knows whether you have come to royal position for such a time as this?*" (Esther 4:13)

It's time! Multitudes around the nations have heard these two words uttered—and usually at the most seemingly inopportune time—from a pregnant woman whose water has broken, signaling the birth of her baby. There have been previous months of waiting, while gestation was taking place, in order to bring about this moment of time! Time, in this sense, means a favourable or appointed time. When a pregnant woman's water breaks and she begins to go into labour, there is no more time to wait. The time decided on beforehand and designated as the moment has arrived; it is happening now. It's time.

In my local church, we have recently had multiple babies born, and still have three more on the way in the next few months. In fact, as I write this, one of our pastors is due to have her baby today! The allotted time of gestation is nearing the end, and the *favourable* and *appointed time* is about to come upon her. The designated nine months of gestation is finished; it's happening now. Soon there will be a brand new little life before our eyes—an amazing miracle of God!

Biblically, we know that God established, before the foundations of the earth were created, designated favourable and appointed times for a variety of earthly events. I could quote and mention multiple set times from the Bible, but just to mention two, we have the births of John the Baptist and Jesus. The Bible also speaks of a favourable and appointed time for Christ's return to earth, gathering home all of the redeemed. Reading from the book of Esther, we also see an appointed time, pre-designated by our Heavenly Father, in which Esther would rise to a place in her culture where she would be asked to stand in the gap on behalf of her Jewish people, thwarting the annihilation of a nation.

In the biblical account of Esther, we find her rising to prominence after King Xerxes issues a royal decree that his present queen, Vashti, is to be banned from ever entering his presence again. This verdict was issued due to her disobedience of the King's request to come before him and his guests, that they might look upon her beauty. After the King's anger subsided, he became lonely and, through the advice of his personal attendants, issued an order to have all of the beautiful girls in the land, under Persian rule, brought before him in order to find another Queen. Esther, originally Hadassah, who was being brought up by her cousin Mordecai, having been orphaned, was one of the girls chosen to be in the King's harem. She was placed under the care of the King's eunuch, Hegai. Esther pleased Hegai, and won his favour; thus he immediately provided her with beauty treatments, special food, the best place in the harem, and seven attending maids. During this time, Esther did not reveal her Jewish heritage, as Mordecai had forbidden her to do so. When the time came for her to go before the King, she did all that Hegai told her to do and, therefore, won the favour of King Xerxes over all the other girls. He placed a royal crown upon her head, making her Queen of Persia in place of Vashti.

During this time, Mordecai, Esther's cousin, who held a high position in the civil service of the Persian Empire, overheard a plot to assassinate King Xerxes. Mordecai reported the plot to Queen Esther, who in turn reported it to the king and the plot was thwarted.

About four years later, a man by the name of Haman is elevated to a seat of honour, higher than all of the nobles. At the king's gate, all of the nobles knelt down by command of the king before Haman, except Mordecai. This happened day after day, and it enraged Haman. Discovering that Mordecai was a Jew, he plotted not only to kill Mordecai, but a way to destroy all of the Jews throughout the Persian Empire. This plot was brought before the King, under the guise of it not be in the king's best interest to have people in the land with differing customs than he. Therefore, the king issued a decree on Haman's advice to annihilate the Jews.

After the edict was issued to all of the Jews in the land, Mordecai sent a copy of the edict to Queen Esther, asking her to intervene on their behalf. Conversing with Mordecai through one of the king's eunuchs, Queen Esther hesitated in going before the king, as he hadn't asked her to come to him for thirty days. She knew that there was only one law for those who approached the inner court of the king without having been summoned: death. Mordecai responded with this exhortation:

> *Do not think that because you are in the king's house you alone of all the Jews will escape. For if you remain silent at this time, relief and deliverance will arise from another place, but you and your father's family will perish. And who knows but that you have come to royal position for such a time as this?* (Esther 4:13–14)

Queen Esther responded to Mordecai that he should gather all the Jews together to fast for three days, and after this fast she would go before the king, even though it was against the law, and if she perished, she perished.

Queen Esther went before the king, dressed in her royal robes, and because the king was pleased with her he extended the gold scepter, asking her request. Esther invited the king to three different banquets, three days in a row, including the wicked Haman. During the third banquet, Esther revealed the wicked plot of Haman to annihilate the Jews, and thus the plot was thwarted.

In light of God's panoramic view discussed in the last chapter, what can we draw from the book of Esther that can be applied in our day, and in our time? In this biblical account, we find that it wasn't until Esther had come into the most intimate of relationships with the king, as his wife and queen, that she was able to *effectively* intercede for her Jewish people and thwart the plans of the enemy to have them all annihilated. It was through her intimacy and favour with the king that she was extended the royal scepter, which showed she was not to be punished, was allowed to speak, and she would receive her request of the king.

If we look at this story as Esther representing the church, we can draw out the principle that we need to be in the most intimate of walks with Jesus, our heavenly king, that we might come before Him, into His inner courts. Through His pleasure with us we will find favour because of our inner beauty of a pure heart, holiness of character, and clean hands, wearing the priestly robes of righteousness provided by Jesus Christ. Our favour with the king will allow us to *effectively* intercede on behalf of the Jewish nation, that they might have the blinders removed from their eyes, and turn and receive salvation.

Is it possible that we, the universal church, *have come to our royal position for such a time as this,* a *favourable* and *appointed* time? However, we need not tremble and fast, as Esther did, in fear of dying for going before the king, without being summoned. Through the crucifixion and death of Jesus Christ, because of His shed blood and His resurrection on the third day, and His ascension to sit at the right hand of the Father in heaven, we can boldly go before the king's throne and enter into His inner courts, presenting our requests before Him. The summons to enter His courts has already been issued through Christ. The only requirement is that we are walking in intimacy with Jesus, and wearing our robes of righteousness that are pure, unspotted, and clean. My question is, can we say that this is what our robes of righteousness look like, unspotted, unblemished, unwrinkled? Ephesians 5:27 says, *"...and to present her to himself as a radiant church, without stain or wrinkle or any other blemish, but holy and blameless."* Are we radiant, without stain, blemish or wrinkle? Are you, personally? May I just say here that the smallest of sins will, if left unchecked and not dealt with, become a major blemish in the sight of God and cause Him to lift His presence from one's personal temple, a local church, or the corporate and universal body of Christ.

Last weekend, as I was driving home from attending a seminar, I spotted a lone Styrofoam coffee cup lying in the middle of the road. Someone had obviously thrown it out of his or her vehicle. As I was driving by, I felt the prompting of the Holy Spirit to stop and pick it up. Admittedly, I said, "Really, God, you want me to pick up that one coffee cup?" His response was a definite yes. I immediately stopped and turned my car around, knowing that He desired to teach me something. This road, as far as I could tell, was completely free of any garbage, and my eye was immediately removed from all of the beauty of nature that was around me, and focused in on that one piece of garbage. The principle He reminded me of was that if I didn't pick up that one piece of garbage, then the next person driving by may feel it's okay to chuck their coffee cup out the window, and or simply not pick it up either, and so on. Carried to the extreme, this principle would suggest that in a little while that road could potentially be filled with garbage. Extreme example? Perhaps, but it gets the point across that in order to stop something from growing to be a larger problem, it needs to be dealt with at the *very first appearance*.

Acknowledging this principle, there is a particular sin that God desires to deal with in the nations of the world, but in order for Him to deal with it in the nations, He first has to deal with it in His people, the church, who are called by His Name. For His Name's sake, it is crucial He deal with this sin because it is bringing shame on the body of Christ, and shame on the nations of the world. God did not create us for shame. He created us for glory!

The sin God desires to pluck up and tear down is sexual immorality, in all of its variants, as He views sexual immorality as a serious yeast amongst His people. The Bible says that the body of Christ is not to have even a hint of sexual immorality within its walls. Ephesians 5:3 emphatically states, *"But among you there must not be even a hint of sexual immorality, or of any kind of impurity, or of greed, because these are improper for God's holy people."* Again, in 1 Corinthians 6:18, He says, *"'Flee from sexual immorality. All other sins a man commits are outside his body, but he who sins sexually sins against his own body.'"*

My example above of the lone coffee cup was spoken to me on my drive home from a seminar called *The Justice Summit*, about bringing awareness and ideas for effective activism on the issue of sex trafficking. God was encouraging me to understand that sex trafficking begins with a 'hint' of sexualization and objectification of women and children. It begins with a perspective that it is acceptable to see another human being as less than a whole person, and reduces them to an object—refuse. One lone coffee cup thrown out the window and not cleaned up.

In Leviticus 18, we read about all of the different types of sexual relations declared unlawful for Israel to participate in, as it would defile the land. In this passage, God reminded the Israelites that sexual immorality was the *precise reason* God was driving out the nations before them so they could take over the Promised Land; the inhabitants of that land had defiled it with *unlawful sexual practices*, and thus *even the land* was *defiled and, therefore, vomited out its inhabitants.* (Leviticus 18:25) Do we understand that we are now the promised land of Christ, His resting place, and He is our promised land, our resting place? In the book of Revelation, Jesus tells the Laodicean church that because they were lukewarm and didn't know that they were blind, wretched, pitiful, and poor, He was going to 'vomit' them out of His mouth! Their indifference and apathy to the gospel and their lack of holiness defiled the land. The dictionary defines defiled as being tainted, marred, spoilt, desecrated, profaned, and polluted. Is Christ's Promised Land, the church, being defiled through our participation in unlawful sexual practices that are not proper for the body of Christ? Are we in danger of being vomited out of the mouth of Christ, removed from His presence? Are we corporately able to come before our heavenly king, knowing that because of our intimacy with Him, wearing untainted, unmarred, unspoiled robes of righteousness, we will be heard by Him and granted our request for the salvation of a harvest of Gentiles, and the Jewish remnant?

The Bible tells us in Romans 11:20b–22,

> *Do not be arrogant (Gentiles), but be afraid. For if God did not spare the natural branches (Israel), he will not spare you either. Consider therefore the kindness and sternness of God: sternness to those who fell (Israel), but kindness to you (Gentiles), provided that you continue in his kindness. Otherwise, you also will be cut off.*

God cannot look upon those with unclean hands and impure hearts who are not walking in holiness. The Psalmist declares, *"Who may ascend the hill of the Lord? Who may stand in his holy place? He who has clean hands and a pure heart…"* (Psalm 24:3–4a). God will not hear us if we cherish or hold sin in our hearts. The heavens are shut up and He will not hear us; thus, we will not hear Him, either. Psalm 66:18 states, *"If I had cherished sin in my heart, the Lord would not have listened."* Again in Isaiah 1:15, we read, *"When you spread out your hands in prayer, I will hide my eyes from you; even if you offer many prayers, I will not listen. Your hands are full of blood."*

Can God hear you? Can God see you? Will God listen to your prayers because you are able to stand in His holy place? Do you have clean hands and a pure heart or have you sold out to sexual immorality? Even a hint? Are you cherishing sin in your heart?

What does it mean to cherish sin in your heart? Let me give you an example. Years ago, about two years after I became a Christian, I attended a Conference where the speaker was John Bevere, and his message was on the fear of the Lord. Up to that point, I had never heard nor felt the tangible conviction of God quite like that evening, and it was for one little hint of sin that I seemed to be cherishing in my heart. I didn't know that this one little thing was such a problem to God because I wasn't acting on it in any way, except it was in my heart and every now and then would surface in my thoughts. That night, during his message, John shared a story about a Christian guy who had trouble quitting smoking, although he desired to do so. One night, this guy took a friend to church and his friend was gloriously saved, and delivered from smoking. This guy, although happy about his friend's salvation, was thoroughly upset with God for delivering his friend immediately from smoking, when he was still struggling with it. After having dropped his friend off, he went home and, crying out to God, hollered, "Why haven't you delivered me?" This guy said he heard what seemed like an audible voice say, "Because you still *like* it!" Immediately, this guy's heart melted, he repented, and was immediately delivered! As John Bevere spoke those words, "Because you still *like* it," the same thing happened for me with the hint of sin I'd been cherishing (holding onto in my heart). I realized I couldn't shake the hint of sin because *I still liked it.* I repented, and received God's grace and deliverance that night, and a spirit of the fear of the Lord fell on me and never left.

God's word says if we cherish sin in our hearts, if we still *like* our sin, no matter how much we cry out for deliverance, the deliverance will evade us because we are not truly repentant. We're still cherishing the sin. However, if we will hate our sin, and love righteousness, then He will deliver us and set us free that we may stand in His holy place. He will once again see us, hear us, and listen to us.

2 Chronicles 7:14–16 says,

> *If my people, who are called by my name, will humble themselves and pray and seek my face and turn from their wicked ways, then I will hear from heaven, and I will forgive their sin and will heal their land. Now my eyes will be open and my ears attentive to the prayers offered in this place. I have chosen and consecrated this temple so that my Name may be there forever. My eyes and my heart will always be there.*

three

CASTING OFF RESTRAINTS:
Falling Asleep in the Lap of Sexual Immorality

"Where there is no revelation, people cast off restraints; but blessed is the one who heeds wisdom." (Proverbs 29:18)

The Bible repeatedly warns and exhorts God's people to flee sexual immorality. We readily know of the wisdom chapters in the book of Proverbs that speak, at length, on this issue and the need to flee! We know well 1 Corinthians 6:18, that states, *"Flee sexual immorality. All other sins a man commits are outside his body, but he who sins sexually sins against his own body.* It is interesting to note that the word flee means to run away from a situation or place of danger. When you look up the word danger, you learn it actually comes from the Latin root word *dominus, lord,* meaning *jurisdiction* or power, and specifically *power to harm.*[5]

God says flee sexual immorality because it is the one realm where the enemy takes back jurisdiction and power to harm your body, and your very spirit. This is exceptionally important because as a Christian, and having received salvation, it is your *spirit* that has been made alive again

---

[5] *New Oxford American Dictionary*, Second Edition, Erin McKean (editor), May 2005, Oxford University Press.

in Christ and you are now *"...united as one with Jesus"* (1 Corinthians 6:17). It is through our *regenerated spirit* that we commune with Jesus, through the Holy Spirit. His Spirit takes up residence within *our spirit* and we become one within the spiritual life of the Trinity—the life that exists between the Father, Son, and Holy Spirit. The Bible teaches us that through sexual intercourse with our marriage partner we also become *one in spirit*, which the apostle Paul says is a mystery. However, this is what takes place, and within this marital bond a three-cord strand is created: husband, wife, and the bond of the Holy Spirit, all as *one*. This relationship is representative of Christ and the church, and the bond of the Holy Spirit that connects the two. (1 Corinthians 6:15–20) If one then chooses to engage in sexual immorality, the sin against their own body is that they allow the enemy jurisdiction to cause them harm. The enemy now has legal, authoritative right to make decisions and judgments over your spirit and can now access your very spirit and not just your mind.

If we are living a righteous life, not practicing sin, Satan has to ask God for permission to touch our lives. However, when we practice the sin of sexual immorality, the Holy Spirit has to leave, and our hedge of protection from God is down. We hand our spirit over to Satan.

The Bible reveals that while Adam was in the garden under God's sovereignty, he was delegated full authority, command, dominion, power and jurisdiction over the territory of the garden. However, through his disobedience of God's command to not eat the forbidden fruit, Adam handed his spirit and jurisdiction over to Satan. Adam and Eve, and all of humanity born thereafter, were now spiritually dead and needed to be spiritually reborn. Satan now had the official power to make legal decisions and judgments over Adam and Eve. (Genesis 3) Through Jesus' death and resurrection, He legally took back jurisdiction for those who believe in Christ and once again has given us back all authority, command, dominion, and power over the enemy. (Luke 10:19, 1 Corinthians 15:24, Ephesians 1:21) Our spirits are under God's divine protection and, according to the book of Job, the enemy has to ask God for permission to touch us. In Job 1:12, we find Satan as the accuser of the brethren, standing before the presence of God asking permission to bypass the spiritual hedge around Job and touch his life. In response, God says, "*Very well, then, everything he has is in your hands, but on the man himself do not lay a finger.*" Again, we see in Job 2:6 a conversation between Satan and God in which God again grants Satan measured permission to touch Job's life. "*Very well, then, he is in your hands; but you must spare his life.*"

This principle is also highlighted in Paul's letter to the Corinthian church in 1 Corinthians 5:5. Discussing how the church should deal with the issue of habitual sexual immorality by a believer, Paul states, "*...hand this man over to Satan...*"

Clark's commentary on this scripture[6] states,

> ...It was a species of punishment administered in extraordinary cases, in which the body and the mind of an incorrigible transgressor were delivered by the authority of God into the power of Satan, to be tortured with diseases and terrors as a warning to all; but while the body and mind were thus tormented, the immortal spirit was under the influence of the Divine mercy; and the affliction, in all probability, was in general only for a season; though sometimes it was evidently unto death, as the destruction of the flesh seems to imply...

Let me explain further. For the redeemed, without sexual immorality, the enemy is on the outside looking in (like the wolf in the story of the three little pigs), and can only knock on the door of your mind, and ask for access. He usually gains access to our minds by deceiving us into believing something to be true when it is not. Embracing the lie, we grant him access. This doesn't satisfy him, though, because although he can cause us to live a less than abundant life, we are still spiritually alive to Christ. However, if he can gain access to our regenerated spirit, then he can *make dead* what was once alive to Jesus and can, through us handing over jurisdiction, condemn us once again before God. By handing our spirit back over to Satan through sexual immorality, we

---

[6] *Commentary on the Bible*, by Adam Clarke [1831]. http://clarke.biblecommenter.com/1_corinthians/5.htm

allow the enemy the right to trample on the Son of the Living God who already went to the cross, and was whipped and beaten beyond recognition for *our* sins!

The Bible warns,

> *If we deliberately keep on sinning after we have received the knowledge of the truth, no sacrifice for sins is left, but only fearful expectation of judgment and of raging fire that will consume the enemies of God...How much more severely do you think a man deserves to be punished who has trampled the Son of God underfoot, who has treated as an unholy thing the blood of the covenant that sanctified him, and who has insulted the Spirit of grace?* (Hebrews 10:26–29)

We also read in Hebrews 6:4–8,

> *It is impossible for those who have once been enlightened, who have tasted the heavenly gift, who have shared in the Holy Spirit, who have tasted the goodness of the word of God and the powers of the coming age and have fallen away, to be brought back to repentance.*[7] *To their loss they are crucifying the Son of God all over again and subjecting him to public disgrace.*

Jesus, our Lord and Saviour, who was crucified, buried and dead, and then rose again, *publicly disgraced* the enemy by taking back the keys to death and hell, but through sexual immorality the enemy is allowed to instead *publicly disgrace* our Saviour!

1 Corinthians 6:13b–15 says,

> *...The body, however, is not meant for sexual immorality but for the Lord, and the Lord for the body. By his power God raised the*

[7] One can only come to repentance by the drawing of the Holy Spirit. If conviction has been brought with no fruits of repentance following, then the Holy Spirit withdraws and there is no more grace—only judgment. Only God can decide when this has occurred.

Lord from the dead, and he will raise us also. Do you not know that your bodies are members of Christ himself? Shall I then take the members of Christ and unite them with a prostitute? Never!

Oh, dear God! Flee sexual immorality! 1 Corinthians 6:19 states, *"Do you not know that your bodies are temples of the Holy Spirit, who is in you, whom you received from God? You are not your own; you were bought at a price. Therefore, honour God with your bodies."* Repent, turn, and get back under the spirit of grace! God will forgive, but you have to heed His warning now. Now is the proper season to heed this warning: *if you deliberately keep on sinning after having received the knowledge of the truth, there is no sacrifice left, there will be no grace; only judgment!*

The *conscience* of the church must be awakened, for it has fallen asleep in the lap of sexual immorality! Conscience, when it is broken down, means "with knowledge." Con meaning "with" and science meaning "knowledge." So, with knowledge, many say they are Christian and sit in a pew, Sunday after Sunday, but from Monday to Saturday deliberately engage in some form of sexual immorality. Therefore, their conscience is being seared and hardened and is asleep while the devil is awake, actively seeking whom he may devour. I am not going to spell out in detail what kind of sexual immorality that might be for you; that could only lead to legalism and thoughts like, *how close can I get to the line of sexual immorality and still avoid judgment?* You know what has risen in your heart, and what the Spirit of God is convicting you of; it is *that* from which He wants you to repent. Don't let your conscience become seared by continuing to sin with knowledge of the truth. Instead, get so on fire for God, and so in love with Jesus, that you will desire to be as far away from the line of sexual immorality as you can possibly be. Don't think you can heap coals into your lap and not get burned! (Proverbs 6:27)

There are multiple scriptures concerning sin, and sexual immorality is the very first sin listed in each. 1 Corinthians 5:9–11 says, "*You must not associate with anyone who claims to be a brother or sister but is sexually immoral…* "and 1 Corinthians 6:9–11 states, *"Do not be deceived: Neither the sexually immoral…will inherit the kingdom of God."* In Galatians

5:19 we read, *"The acts of the flesh are obvious: (those who practice) sexual immorality,...(and) orgies...I warn you, as I did before, that those who live like this will not inherit the kingdom of God."* Sexual immorality takes top position again in Colossians 3:5, *"Put to death, therefore, whatever belongs to your earthly nature: sexual immorality..."* God's word is emphatic with warnings about sexual immorality. He says, don't be deceived—you will not inherit the kingdom of God. Put sexual immorality to death! Don't let it live in you. Deuteronomy 30:19 says, *"I have set before you life and death, blessings and curses. Now choose life."*

Let's look at two biblical examples and *representations of the church*, and how they handled sexual immorality and the outcome of both. One *representation* is blessed, and heeds wisdom; the other *representation* is without revelation and casts off restraints.

First is the story of Joseph. If we have grown up in church, we have heard it repeatedly in Sunday school. Joseph was the second-youngest and favourite son—out of the twelve—of Jacob, and was given a coat of many colours, which symbolized favour. As a boy, Joseph, was given a dream by God concerning his future, and because of jealousy and envy of his brothers, he was thrown into a pit, and then sold into slavery and taken to Egypt. Joseph, because of God's favour on his life, rose to be head servant in the household of Potiphar, the head of the palace guard. Potiphar's wife, however, found the favour of God on Joseph attractive, and tried desperately, day after day, to seduce him. Joseph, however, fearing God, and knowing the scriptures, literally fled sexual immorality by running away from Potiphar's wife during one of her attempts at getting him to lay with her. In her anger at being rebuffed, Potiphar's wife ripped Joseph's robe from him and cried rape. Joseph was thrown into prison, where he remained for two or more years before being released by the Pharaoh of Egypt, who had come to understand that Joseph was adept at interpreting dreams. Joseph then rose in favour with Pharaoh and became the Lord of Pharaoh's house. Joseph's wisdom, stewardship, and prominence in Pharaoh's house, allowed him to oversee Egypt's storehouses during a desperate famine in the land of his father, Jacob, and his brothers. Through a series of events, the story concludes with Joseph being restored to his brothers and his father, Jacob, thus bringing about the deliverance, salvation, and protection of the nation of Israel. (Genesis 37:1–36; 39–47)

If we briefly examine this story of Joseph through the lens of him representing the church, we can extract the principles that the enemy was desperately trying to strip the favour of God from Joseph through sexual immorality. He knew that if he could strip Joseph of his intimate relationship with God, then his protection would be gone and the nation of Israel would starve during the famine, and would not be delivered and preserved. Joseph's example is how the church is to correctly handle the temptation of sexual immorality when it presents itself, as sexual immorality is the opposite of being in intimacy with God and leaves us weak, vulnerable, and without vision. It will leave us to starve through a famine of God's word and presence, and once again the Jewish nation will not be delivered or saved!

In the Old Testament, we constantly see the nation of Israel walking in the blessings of God, and then falling into disobedience and losing their protection and blessings through engaging in sexual immorality with the nations around them. God was constantly warning His people and then having to bring judgment upon them for not listening to His voice of warning to flee sexual immorality.

If we take a moment to look at the story of Samson in the book of Judges, we notice that he was a chosen vessel by God before his birth to become a Nazarite, separated and consecrated to God for His eternal purposes within the Israelite nation. God's purpose was to begin to bring the Israelites deliverance from the oppressive Philistines. Samson, because of his call of separation unto God, and the anointing resting upon his life to do great exploits, was exceptionally strong. This strength and anointing was not for him, but was for helping to bring freedom to his people by fighting against the Philistines. As we read, we notice Samson, because of a loss of purpose and God's vision for his life, casting off restraints by engaging his fleshly distractions with prostitutes and ultimately Delilah. This whole scenario suggests sexual immorality, which was strictly forbidden for the nation Israel, let alone Samson, a Nazarite. The Bible tells us that Samson falls asleep in the lap of Delilah and, having already shared with her that the length of his hair was the secret of his strength, wakes up to find his hair cut and his strength and anointing of God gone. Samson is left vulnerable and weak before the Philistines, and they come and gouge out his eyes, carrying him into slavery and bondage. Samson, who was to bring the beginning of deliverance to Israel from their oppression, leaves them *still* oppressed by the Philistines. (Judges 13–16)

My question for us as the Gentile church would be: have we not been left vulnerable and weak because we have lost the prophetic vision? A prophetic vision of deep intimacy with Jesus, and having His glory revealed in us that the Jewish nation might be freed from the enemy that oppresses them—the enemy that keeps them blinded from having their eyes opened that they might see their Messiah, turn, and be saved? Have we not cast off restraints and allowed more than a hint of sexual immorality into our midst to feed our fleshly desires that we now, like Samson, have fallen asleep in the lap of sexual immorality and become weakened and vulnerable? Have we not allowed the enemy access to come and gouge out our eyes that we would have no vision, and be brought into slavery and bondage? Thus the fullness of the Gentiles has not been brought into salvation and intimacy with Christ and, therefore, the Jews are still not saved? (Romans 9:1–5)

So what do we do? The prophetic vision must be restored in its fullness to the Gentile church. After he was in slavery and bondage for a time, Samson called out to God, repented, and asked God to, *once again,* empower him with strength—to anoint him one more time.

> *Then Samson prayed to the LORD, "O Sovereign LORD, remember me. O God, please strengthen me just once more, and let me with one blow get revenge on the Philistines for my two eyes." Then Samson reached toward the two central pillars on which the temple stood. Bracing himself against them, his right hand on the one and his left hand on the other, Samson said, "Let me die with the Philistines!" Then he pushed with all his might, and down came the temple on the rulers and all the people in it. Thus he killed many more when he died than while he lived."*

We can glean a spiritual principle from this passage that God would voice to us today:

> Church, if you will call out to me, repent, and turn from all of your wickedness—if you will let me kill your fleshly desires, then you will see more of the enemy's activities die within those to whom you minister than you saw in your lives when you thought you were living.

Then, *"I will once more shake the heavens and the earth, the sea and the dry land. I will shake all nations, and the desired of all nations will come, and I will fill this house with glory,' says the LORD Almighty"* (Haggai 2:6–7, emphasis added).

Even so, Come, Lord Jesus, Come!

I will draw perspective from one more representation of the church in the Bible. This representation is *not* how *we* are to deal with sexual immorality, but *how Jesus deals with us* when it is exposed in the church. Again, so I do not lose the poignancy of the passage, I am going to include it in full.

> *But Jesus went to the Mount of Olives. At dawn he appeared again in the temple courts, where all the people gathered around him, and he sat down to teach them. The teachers of the law and the Pharisees brought in a woman caught in adultery. They made her stand before the group and said to Jesus, "Teacher, this woman was caught in the act of adultery. In the Law Moses commanded us to stone such women. Now what do you say?" They were using this question as a trap, in order to have a basis for accusing him.*
>
> *But Jesus bent down and started to write on the ground with his finger. When they kept on questioning him, he straightened up and said to them, "Let any one of you who is without sin be the first to throw a stone at her." Again he stooped down and wrote on the ground.*
>
> *At this, those who heard began to go away one at a time, the older ones first, until only Jesus was left, with the woman still standing*

> *there. Jesus straightened up and asked her, "Woman, where are they? Has no one condemned you?" "No one, sir," she said. "Then neither do I condemn you," Jesus declared. "Go now and leave your life of sin."* (John 8:1–11)

In 2006, I started a painting I plan to call *Grace*. It represents Jesus kneeling and writing in the sand. In the painting, I have positioned Jesus right at the forefront, encompassing the majority of the canvas space. I did this to represent that in this story of the woman caught in adultery, the Pharisees, who represented the Old Covenant and the law of Moses, and legalism (as the Pharisees had carried the laws too far), were being moved to the background, and grace through Jesus Christ and the New Covenant was coming to the forefront. The background is painted as the dawn, as in the scripture passage, signifying the dawning of a new day, the dawning of the church era and grace. I will finish the painting now, as I believe it to be a prophetic picture of what Jesus is about to do in His church.

The church, like the woman in this passage, has been caught engaging in sexual immorality, and the enemy has been thrusting the church before Jesus Christ and condemning her in the temple courts. However, because of God's grace through His shed blood on the Cross, *if there is repentance*, He will quickly forgive her sin, and the dawn of a new day will appear for the church.

four

INNOCENCE COMPROMISED:
Consequence of Sexual Immorality

"Be self-controlled and alert. Your enemy the devil prowls around like a roaring lion looking for someone to devour." (1 Peter 5:8)

God is a covenant-keeping God. He always keeps His promises, as He cannot lie. The Bible says let every man be found a liar, but not Him! Not only is He a covenant-keeping God, He is a generational God. He is the same God yesterday, today, and forever! His promises are the same yesterday, today, and forever. Therefore, God keeps His covenants and promises to yesterday's generation, today's generation, and to tomorrow's generation! His covenants and promises have never been declared to one generation only; He always declared His covenants and promises to the current age, including future generations. Let me cite a few examples.

First, we have Adam and Eve and the Edenic Covenant—be fruitful and multiply, bring forth generations.

> *God blessed them and said to them, "Be fruitful and increase in number; fill the earth and subdue it. Rule over the fish of the sea and the birds of the air and over every living creature that moves on the ground."* (Genesis 1:28)

Next came Noah and the Noahic Covenant, echoing: be fruitful and multiply.

> *"Be fruitful and increase in number and fill the earth...I now establish my covenant with you and with your descendants after you...This is the sign of the covenant I am making between me and you and every living creature with you, a covenant for all generations to come..."* (Genesis 9:1–12)

Then we read of Abraham and the Abrahamic Covenant—God's promise to give Abraham land, children and descendants:

> *I will make you into a great nation, and I will bless you; I will make your name great, and you will be a blessing. I will bless those who bless you, and whoever curses you I will curse; and all peoples on earth will be blessed through you.* (Genesis 12:2–3)

God reiterated His covenant with Abraham to Isaac and to Jacob. Then we have the Mosaic Covenant—these commands apply to you and your descendants:

> *These are the commands, decrees and laws the Lord your God directed me to teach you to observe in the land that you are crossing the Jordan to possess, so that you, your children and their children after them may fear the Lord your God as long as you live by keeping all his decrees and commands that I give you, and so that you may enjoy long life. Hear, Israel, and be careful to obey so that it may go well with you and that you may increase greatly in a land flowing with milk and honey, just as the Lord, the God of your ancestors, promised you.* (Deuteronomy 6:1–3)

Moses reminds Israel of the covenant just before entering the Promised Land—this covenant is not with you alone:

a covenant the Lord is making with you this day and sealing with an oath, to confirm you this day as his people, that he may be your God as he promised you and as he swore to your fathers, Abraham, Isaac and Jacob. I am making this covenant, with its oath, not only with you who are standing here with us today in the presence of the Lord our God but also with those who are not here today. (Deuteronomy 29:12–15)

Acts—the promise of the gift of the Holy Spirit for all who believe:

Peter replied, "Repent and be baptized, every one of you, in the name of Jesus Christ for the forgiveness of your sins. And you will receive the gift of the Holy Spirit. The promise is for you and your children and for all who are far off—for all whom the Lord our God will call." (Acts 2:38–39)

Moses exhorts Israel:

The Lord did not set his affection on you and choose you because you were more numerous than other peoples, for you were the fewest of all peoples. But it was because the Lord loved you and kept the oath he swore to your ancestors that he brought you out with a mighty hand and redeemed you from the land of slavery, from the power of Pharaoh king of Egypt. Know therefore that the Lord your God is God; he is the faithful God, keeping his covenant of love to a thousand generations of those who love him and keep his commandments. (Deuteronomy 7:7–9)

As we can see, God is a covenant God, a promise-keeping God, and a generational God. He thinks generationally, therefore so must we. As covenant children, we need to inspect some walls that are broken down and leaving our children unprotected and vulnerable to the enemy. Like Nehemiah, we need to come in proximity to the ruins that we might perceive and understand the need to rebuild the walls of protection around the next generation.

In my home office I have a picture on my wall of a grandfather's clasped hands held as if in prayer. In between his arms, and leaning with head bowed and arms draped over his hands, is a one-year-old grandchild. The saying on the picture is, "The hope of future generations rests in our hands. May we keep that in our hearts" (Anonymous).

Another quote that inspired me continuously when I was beginning to hear and respond to God's call to speak out on behalf of the sexualization and objectification of women and children in our society and the connection it has to sex trafficking, is this: "Never forsake what you are called to do today, for tomorrow it will change the future of your children and your descendants" (Author Unknown).

In the first three chapters, we allowed God to determine where the enemy, through sexual immorality, has been permitted access to our lives, and now we must allow Him access to examine the devastating consequences. The consequences of sexual immorality and our silence concerning sexual immorality is the compromise of innocent children, and through this compromise the enemy is devouring them.

This chapter is exceptionally weighty for me to write. It is particularly close to my heart, and if anything can stir up righteous anger in me, it is children being compromised. To compromise our children means to undermine, weaken, damage, jeopardize, dishonour, shame, or embarrass them. I believe our innocent children are being severely compromised through diverse forms of overt, continuous, negative sexualized media. It is my assertion that a society that compromises the innocent compromises itself, and a society that does not protect the innocent is abhorrent. Further, to compromise and not *protect* the innocent for *our entertainment*—for example, the television show *Toddlers and Tiaras*—is reprehensible. We violate the rights of vulnerable children, whom we are responsible to protect. We gamble with the value of our children's innocence, hindering their ability to fulfill their potential.

John Wesley used to say, "What one generation tolerates, the next generation will embrace." A portion of our generation of Christians is tolerating, engaging in, and even promoting sexual immorality through behaviours and silence. We are silent because we engage in these behaviours ourselves; are afraid of being called prudes, old fashioned, narrow minded, dogmatic, or now homophobic; or don't believe we can make a difference. Because of this, the next generation will embrace sexual immorality, believing it not to be a problem. To embrace something means to give it willing support, to encircle, surround, and enclose. The next generation, then, if they embrace sexual immorality will be encircling, surrounding and enclosing shame instead of glory!

THE MESSAGE OF SILENCE:

Proverbs 31:8 says, *"Speak up for those who cannot speak for themselves…"* Silence has a voice and transmits a message. The message of silence can be understood as consent or ambivalence. With a mere absence of mention, silence suggests that either one agrees with what is taking place, or one does not care. It gives a collective nod to the behaviours and can be a collaborator of abuse. The voice of silence speaks louder, longer, and deeper than even the spoken word. Silence can scar a heart, encourage behaviour, or oppress a thought, word, or action. Silence can promote, permit, or condone. Silence can have a profound influence and an effect far beyond an action or behaviour. For example, an abuse victim, after having gone through a healing process of dealing with abuse (mental, emotional, physical, or sexual), will have to turn and deal with the intense hurt and emotional turmoil over why those present and aware didn't do or say something. Why didn't they speak up or take action to stop the abuse?

We are being silent and absent (or at least not vocal enough) concerning the effects and consequences that sexualization and objectification of women and children in the media is having on our children. What society is experiencing with the sex-trafficking issue, and what we will experience in the next two generations, is and will be unprecedented. Technology places us in a position of abusing a whole generation of children through a bombardment of continuous, repetitive, negative sexualized media. We are potentially mentally sexually abusing every single child, male and female, in our western society, through the onslaught of continuous, negative sexualized media. We are promoting and permitting the acceptability of sexualization and objectification of women and children and, subtly encouraged by our silence, a rise of the acceptability of soft pornography where innocent children have access.

As I write this chapter, the very thing I am concerned about is happening right before our eyes in the capital of my nation, Canada. A sex-exhibition under the guise of science has opened at the Canadian Science and Technology Museum. This exhibition promotes, visually and with some vulgar language, multiple sex partners, homosexuality, pornography, masturbation, sex experimentation, and friends with benefits (sexual partners with no commitment or emotional attachment). This exhibition was originally geared to those twelve years of age (with adult accompaniment) and up, but people voiced concerns and the minimum age has been changed to sixteen. Thankfully, they also removed an animated video of a boy and girl masturbating. However, the rest of the exhibit is still there, encouraging the sexual choices stated above as something to explore if one chooses. It is one thing to not return to the Victorian Era (as it is called), when one didn't speak of sexuality openly, but there needs to be a balance. We have just moved from one extreme to the other. The balance is an open, honest conversation about healthy sexuality within the confines of a loving, committed, responsible relationship between a husband and wife.

I have recently seen news reports of the following within mere days of each other: the first sex-trafficker convicted in Canada, arrested in my city after having skipped parole; the sentencing of a man and a woman for abducting, abusing, and murdering a little girl; someone painting a nude portrait of our Prime Minister, which now hangs in our local, family library; the sex exhibition described above; an ex-lover involved in a homosexual relationship found murdered, dismembered, and chopped up; and an ad campaign utilizing a sexualized image of a woman fictionally named Bridgett and sexualized speech to slow speeders down on a bridge in Halifax.

Again, as I write and share the message of this book with those who have asked, I hear stories of sexual abuses happening to young children in schools by their peers, called sexual bullying. Wives are sharing their husbands' struggles with pornography, and parents are sharing their children's struggles with pornography and negative sexualized behaviour.

Society and Christians, by our silence and our inability to speak with authority on these issues, due to engaging in these behaviours ourselves, are allowing *a spirit of sexual immorality to awaken.* This spirit is insatiable and will continue to feed and grow until it overtakes our society to the point where we will share the experience of the culture during the biblical times recorded in the book of Judges. Judges chapter 19 describes a horrific story of a time in Israel's history when there was no king and everyone did what was right in their own eyes. The story is how a Levite (originally from the Levitical priesthood) takes a concubine, and after a time she flees back to her father's house. After four months, the Levite decides to go and bring her back. During their return trip, while staying in a stranger's home for a night, sexually depraved men seek to have sex with the Levite. However, instead of the Levite they are offered the stranger's virgin daughter and the Levite's concubine. The men are told they can abuse the girls any way they want for the night. They end up sexually abusing the Levite's concubine all night until the dawn, when the Levite finds her lying on the doorstep, dead. Scripture then states:

> *When he reached home, he took a knife and cut up his concubine, limb by limb, into twelve parts and sent them into all the areas of Israel. Everyone who saw it said, "Such a thing has never been seen or done, not since the day the Israelites came up out of Egypt. Think about it! Consider it! Tell us what to do!"* (Judges 19:29–30)

To be honest, the commentaries are not adequate concerning this Scripture passage and blame the woman for her prostitution, instead of focusing on how depraved and perverted the culture within Israel had become.

This passage is analogous to the sex-trafficking crisis our culture is experiencing. According to the website of Canadian Member of Parliament Joy Smith:[8]

---

[8] http://www.joysmith.ca/main.asp?fxoid=FXMenu,1&cat_ID=27&sub_ID=90

> Twenty seven million slaves exist in the world today, and an estimated two million people are trafficked each year. UNICEF estimates over one million children, each year, are sold into slavery. Women make up for eighty percent of trafficked victims, and fifty percent are children. The majority of the victims are aged 12–16 but can be as young as five years old. Annual revenues of the slave trade reach 32 billion and are quickly surpassing drug and weapons as the biggest criminal enterprise.

We cannot separate the ideologies we promote in our western society through our media from the extreme end of sexualization and objectification, which is sex trafficking. I do not understand how we think we can stop human sex trafficking when we not only permit but promote that women and girls are objects to be looked at for sexual pleasure, used for sexual pleasure, degraded through sexual speech, and sexually harassed in all forms of media. How can we be fighting sex trafficking on one hand, and on the other hand be legalizing brothels in my nation of Canada?

Sexual immorality is subtle and insidious; it creeps in unnoticed and it infiltrates what should be healthy sexual boundaries of innocent children. A hint of sexual immorality is serious because as it increases it touches even the children of a society. Normalizing negative sexual behaviour will create a constraining, addictive, consuming presence in our society that will drown out, water down, and weaken our children and thus society, through suppression of original thought. We will stagnate as a society, entranced in a pleasure stupor, and stop moving forward, which will be our destruction. Once again, the enemy is trying to devour our children before they rise to their authoritative places in Christ, advancing the kingdom of God on earth. There are only two kingdoms advancing on earth: either the enemy's kingdom of darkness, or the kingdom of God, of light.

Sexual immorality is already touching our youngest children. When I previously ran a home daycare, I received age-inappropriate sexual questions and witnessed inappropriate sexual behaviours from four-year-olds. Questions while playing house, like, "Can I kiss her on the lips?" and "Can I lie on top of her?" referring to mimicking intercourse. Recently, I spoke with a woman who experienced a similar scenario during her young child's birthday party. During the festivities, a couple of the children snuck off to another room and removed their clothes. Thankfully, there were watchful eyes and it was interrupted very quickly, but this shouldn't be happening. What are our children viewing and experiencing? The innocence of our youngest children is being stripped from them, whether parents and guardians want it or not. Sexual immorality is rampant, and it is difficult to shield young children from its clutches. Another example I found disturbing not only because it was in an animated movie but also because some adults I shared my concerns with didn't seem to see the problem. They said, "It just goes over their head." Perhaps in some cases such as verbal innuendos, but this scenario utilized an easily recognizable visual symbol. Children retain visual cues quickly, especially if they view the symbol frequently. Let me share the full story with you.

One weekend before Easter, my family decided to watch a G-rated movie called *Hop*. The story is about a bunny growing up expected to take over the family business of making and distributing Easter goodies to all the children of the world. He doesn't want to run the family business, though. He wants to be a drummer. The night he is to officially take over the business from his father, he decides to run away to Hollywood and follow his dream of being in the music business.

So far, none of this is an issue; it's just a cute little story. However, the moment he arrives in Hollywood, he seeks shelter at the "Playboy Bunny" Mansion. There is a big Playboy Bunny logo on the gates of the mansion, and in a desperate hope to gain entrance he tries to convince the gatekeeper to allow him access because he is "so sexy"! This all plays out in a supposedly humorous way.

This is not humorous! What are the Playboy Bunny logo, Playboy Bunny Mansion, and the word sexy doing in a child's G-rated animated movie? As parents and responsible adults, we need to pay *conscious* and *collective* attention to this insidious marketing toward the acceptability of pornography within our children's media. I use the word insidious because it means to proceed in a gradual, subtle way, but with harmful effects. Do we want our innocent children recognizing the Playboy Bunny logo, which points to pornography, on sight? Do we want our children encouraged to believe the symbol is innocuous because it is allowed in their animated movies?

Another example of this insidious form of marketing, which encourages and grooms our children toward negative and premature sexuality, is on the backside of jean pockets from GRG DNM marketed to young girls. When you turn the jeans inside out to launder them, you find this:

Be yourself. Be cool. Be smart. Be hot. 'Be SEXY'...

When did being hot and being sexy become appropriate encouragement for young girls and teens toward becoming all you can be, and fulfilling their full potential in life? The individuals I hear being told to be hot and be sexy are vulnerable women and children who have been forced into prostitution and exploited in the sex-trafficking crisis.

Perhaps we need to take a step back and consider what victims of sex trafficking would say to our western society if they viewed the Playboy Bunny logo and words like sexy in a child's animated movie? Do we think they would pass it off as no big deal? Do we think they would say there is no harm having a symbol that represents pornography in our children's movies? Or do we think they would caution us that we are feeding something that will potentially leave our children vulnerable to exploitation?

Perhaps you are still thinking, "Rachel, you're making a mountain out of a molehill," or that it's not a big deal? Let me ask you this: if you had a three-year-old, and you wanted to read them a bedtime story, would you go to your child's bookshelf and choose a children's book with the Playboy Bunny logo? Would you have bought the book, if it were available? Would you ever think of allowing the sexual innuendos, and images showing up in children's movies, in your child's storybook? Reverend Keith Collins states, "We have become so inoculated to evil that we have become numb to its stinging bite." Are we so desensitized to the negative sexualized media that we no longer see it as a problem, even as Christians? God's word plainly and emphatically states in Matthew 18:6: *"But if anyone causes one of these little ones who believe in me to sin, it would be better for him to have a large millstone hung around his neck and to be drowned in the depths of the sea."*

COMPROMISE BEGETS COMPROMISE

Biblically, we have read it often in the Old Testament genealogies, "and so and so beget so and so..." To beget means to bring into existence by the process of reproduction, give rise to, or bring about. We also know and understand the principle of reaping what we sow. As the Bible warns us, *"Do not be deceived: God cannot be mocked. A man reaps what he sows. The one who sows to please his sinful nature, from that nature will reap destruction; the one who sows to please the Spirit, from the Spirit will reap eternal life."* (Galatians 6:7–8)

Through our compromise with sexual immorality, is it possible that we are compromising our children? Are we enabling the reproduction of this spirit of sexual immorality and aiding its rise? Are we already reaping what we have sown? Will we reap even more devastation in the years to come because of what our generations are sowing now?

A SPIRITUAL LESSON ON COMPROMISE

Years ago, as I was driving home one night, the Holy Spirit spoke the word "Desert" to me. It was so emphatic I had to pull the car over and sit in His presence awhile, before I could continue home. The scriptures talk about God alluring Israel into the desert, that He might speak kindly to her. Well, God sure allured me into a desert experience and His refining fires for the next seven years. Thankfully, God did provide streams in the desert to refresh me, but mentally, emotionally, physically, and spiritually, I was in God's refining fires through a desert experience.

At the very beginning of my desert experience, God began to deal with me about compromise and lukewarmness, and to question me about whom I was going to serve—Baal or the Lord. God has a different view of compromise and what it means to be lukewarm. His thoughts are not our thoughts, and His ways are not our ways. If you would have asked any member of my church, at that time, who was on fire for God, they would have said one of them was me. And I was, but God sees the deepest attitudes of our hearts and will not tolerate or make room for any of our compromises or idols.

During this period, a scripture in Deuteronomy 30:17–18 challenged me. It says:

> *But if your heart turns away (becomes complacent/lukewarm) and you are not obedient (deaf to God's conviction and direction), and if you are drawn away to bow down to other gods (family, social status, etc.) and worship them (choose their acceptance more precious than God's), I declare to you this day that you will certainly be destroyed. You will not live long in the land you are crossing the Jordan to enter and possess.* (Parenthesis mine)

God was dealing with me concerning a small compromise I was making in my family. I won't describe the scenario, because it is more about the attitude of compromise more than the actual event.

May I ask you, just as God challenged me, has your heart turned away from God through compromise and become complacent and lukewarm? Are your eyes, ears, and heart blinded and deaf to His voice, causing you to justify your sin of compromise before a holy God with whom you are in covenant? Have you been drawn away through compromise to bow down to another, such as family members, social status, or acceptance from society? Are you participating in crude jokes at work so that you seem to fit in? Is your chosen career causing you to compromise your purity, physically, mentally or spiritually? What are you placing before your eyes every night? Is it a worldly sitcom like *Two and Half Men*, *How I Met Your Mother*, or *The Big Bang Theory*? Are you finding yourself watching and laughing at these entertaining shows right along with your children, so they don't think you're a prude? Have you become deaf to God's conviction and direction for your life? Are you worshiping someone else because you choose his or her acceptance as more precious than God's? God declares to you this day that you will certainly be destroyed. Destroy is a general term covering any force that wrecks, ruins, kills, etc. I know a thief who comes to steal and kill and destroy: the enemy. God's Word says that there are consequences to compromise. He will lift His presence and protection from our children and us, leaving the enemy access to destroy our homes. Have we compromised with sexual immorality, causing God to leave us to the enemy?

Compromise means two things: first, it means we forfeit the promises of God (the covenant blessings) for our children and us. To forfeit something means you lose or are deprived of a right or privilege, in this case as a consequence for wrongdoing. We can potentially lose our and our children's covenant blessings and inheritance through Christ. Second, compromise has this attitude behind it from Numbers 14:3 (parentheses mine: *"Why is the Lord bringing us to this land (Christianity) only to let us fall by the sword? Our wives (or husbands) and children will be taken as plunder. Wouldn't it be better for us to go back to Egypt (the world)?"*

With this perhaps-unconscious thought we reason, "Why did I enter Christianity just to see my spouse, children, family, friends, and coworkers seemingly not love me, and not enjoy being with me anymore?" "Maybe it would be better if I just relaxed a little in some areas. I am not giving up following Jesus; I am just going to give some slack in this area." Please don't misunderstand me, some aspects within our Christian walk do require discernment whether we are being legalistic and without grace or are truly compromising God's Word in a desire to be accepted. However, if we keep our hearts soft and pliable, and seek God's will, He will convict us when we start to stray or veer off the path. Is God convicting you?

Moses proclaimed to the Israelites the scripture Deuteronomy 30:17–18, quoted earlier, during a renewal of God's covenant promises and curses just before they entered the Promised Land. Moses reminded the Israelites of all God had done for them by delivering them from Egypt, and aiding and providing for them while crossing the desert. Moses declared they were standing, as one nation, in the presence of the LORD their God. He personalized the covenant to every individual by identifying head leaders, down to husbands, wives, children, and even the foreigners (aliens) living with them as servants. Declaring that they were standing before the Lord their God to enter into a covenant, a covenant the Lord their God was making with them, and sealing with an oath. This covenant, sealed with an oath, would confirm that the Lord was *their God* and He would make them *His people* as He had promised them and their fathers, Abraham, Isaac and Jacob. He goes on to say, in Deuteronomy 29:14–15, *"I am making this covenant, with its oath, not only with you who are standing here with us today in the presence of the LORD our God but also with those who are not here today."*

One of the Bible commentaries states,[9] "This covenant Moses made not only with those who were present, but with all whether present or not; for it was to embrace not only those who were living then, but their descendants also, to become a covenant blessing for all nations as seen in Acts 2:39." Another commentary reads, "Not only you, but those that will come after you, your sons and your sons' sons." The covenant blessings and curses apply to future generations.

Moses continued to expound to the Israelites how they saw the idols other nations worshiped as they passed through their lands, arriving where they were standing to take the covenant. They were to make sure no one would turn their hearts away from the Lord their God to go and worship the gods of those nations. Moses then warned those who might become complacent because of the blessings, although they had also heard the curses, and think to themselves, *"I will be safe, even though I persist in going my own way"* (Deuteronomy 29:19a). Moses declared that the curses *would* come upon *them and their children* who followed them. Later generations would wonder at the devastation and desolation of the land, as it would be like the destruction of Sodom and Gomorrah. These other generations would ask, *"Why has the LORD done this to this land?"* And the answer will be: *"It is because this people abandoned the covenant of the LORD...the covenant he made with them when he brought them out of Egypt. They went off and worshiped other gods and bowed down to them, gods they did not know, gods he had not given them"* (Deuteronomy 29:24–26).

Moses then declared that if they did turn away and worship other gods, and the curses came upon them and they were vomited out of

[9] *Biblical Commentary on the Old Testament*, by Carl Friedrich Keil and Franz Delitzsch [1857-78] http://kad.biblecommenter.com

the Promised Land and brought into other lands, God would gather them back and prosper them once again if they would remember their God, repent and turn from their sins. He then promised, *"The LORD your God will circumcise your hearts and the hearts of your descendants, so that you may love him with all your heart and with all your soul, and live"* (Deuteronomy 30:6).

After this, Moses set before the Israelites life and prosperity, death and destruction, blessings and curses. He stated that if they chose blessing and life they would live and increase in the land and God would greatly bless them. But, *"If your heart turns away and you are not obedient, and if you are drawn away to bow down to other gods and worship them, I declare to you this day that you will certainly be destroyed. You will not live long in the land you are crossing the Jordan to enter and possess."* (Deuteronomy 30:15–18)

Moses concluded in verses 19 and 20 with, *"Now choose life, so that you and your children may live and that you may love the LORD your God, listen to his voice, and hold fast to him. For the LORD is your life, and he will give you many years in the land he swore to give to your fathers..."*

Deuteronomy 30:6: "*...The LORD your God will circumcise your hearts and the hearts of your descendants, so that you may love him with all your heart and with all your soul, and live.*"

God Promises that if we will *not* compromise *He will: circumcise our hearts* (circumcision represents God's purifying work) and *take care of making our children, the next generation, holy.* So that *we and our children will love him with all of our hearts,* and that *we may live long in the land.* What a magnificent promise of God!

2 Chronicles 7:14–16 states:

> *If my people, who are called by my name, will humble themselves (repent) and pray and seek my face and turn from their wicked ways, then will I hear from heaven and will forgive their sin and will heal their land. [If you do this] my eyes will be open and my ears attentive to the prayers offered in this place. I have chosen and consecrated this temple so that my Name may be there forever. My eyes and my heart will always be there.* (Parentheses mine)

Do we realize that God has eyes, ears, and a heart that are closed to our prayers if we do not repent and turn from our wicked ways? We have lost our *intimacy* with Christ because of sexual immorality, and God is calling us to *awaken our consciences* once again that we might *turn and awaken the conscience of our society.* There are people, male and female, young and old, crying out to God in desperation to be freed from sexual abuse and exploitation.

Heavenly Father hears their cries for help and deliverance just as He heard the cries of the Israelites when they were in Egypt under deep oppression. When He heard their cries, He sent forth a deliverer on their behalf, Moses. In our day, He sends us forth, His covenant children, to aid in delivering those who are oppressed and without justice. But unlike Moses, we are not prepared. We are unable to deliver because we live without the Deliverer, Jesus! We need to be so intimate with Jesus that we can carry the presence of the Deliverer with us as we go in response to God's call and commission. Are we ready? Can He send us? Are we able to say, "Here I am, Lord, send me"? Can He say, "I have searched for someone to stand in the gap, and I have found a people who can, and will, stand on my behalf"? Are you one He can choose? There are innocent children crying for deliverance!

HEAR US FROM HEAVEN

By Ross Parsley

I Am Free
Lord, hear our cry
Come heal our land
Breathe life into these dry
And thirsty souls
Lord, hear our prayer
Forgive our sins
And as we call on Your name
Would you make this a place for
Your glory to dwell
Open the blind eyes
Unlock the deaf ears
Come to Your people
As we draw near
Hear us from heaven
And touch our generation
We are Your people
Crying out in desperation

SECTION TWO

restoration

five

REFINER'S FIRE:
The Kiln of God's Glory

"'I will shake all nations, and the desired of all nations will come, and I will fill this house with glory,' says the LORD Almighty." (Haggai 2:7)

I believe with all of my heart that God is about to pour out His spirit upon His people in an unprecedented way—bringing us from glory to glory, accelerated until we are immersed in His glory as the disciples were at the dispensation of the church age. We will continue to expand in carrying the glory of God until the kingdom of God is ushered into the earth as it is in heaven. God's Word tells us that deep darkness will be upon the people, but the glory of the LORD will shine upon those who know Him (Isaiah 60:2). I can't think of anything darker than innocent children being abused by sexual immorality in the sex-trafficking crisis. I can't think of anything darker than a western culture protecting, promoting, and engaging in sexualization and objectification of women and children in our media. We are creating a "greenhouse effect" from which sex trafficking is already flourishing. However, I also believe that in the darkest of times, God's glory is going to arise on people who know Him—a people who love and obey His commands. As any artist knows, when you desire to create a highlight that pops in your artwork, you place your lightest light against the darkest dark. God, being the greatest of Artists, is placing His lightest light in society against the darkest dark.

On a personal note, in November 2011, the Holy Spirit began to speak to me about a cellular change happening within the body of Christ. He began to highlight for me the cellular change of a butterfly as it moves from the cocoon stage. There is a complete cellular change—the butterfly, which came from the caterpillar, is entirely different. There are no cellular similarities. Biologist Dr. Lincoln Bower states:[10]

> These little groups of cells (imaginal disks—groups of embryonic cells) start developing very early in the caterpillar's life but then they stall, and so they're just in there waiting, and they don't start growing until the very end of the 5th instar (the last caterpillar stage). Then they start growing really rapidly and differentiating into the different tissues, so that literally the entire internal contents of the caterpillar—the muscles, the entire digestive system, even the heart, even the nervous system—is totally rebuilt. It's like you took your car, a Ford, into the shop and left it there for a week and it came out as a Cadillac.

I believe God is saying there will be an unprecedented move of the Holy Spirit; a complete cellular change within individuals, churches, and communities. A sweep of the Holy Spirit that is not just a transition but a complete cellular change of how we have seen and felt Him move in the past. It will be like the resurrection power that brought Christ back from the dead. People will begin to come to life and walk in resurrection power. I believe strongly that for those who are hungry, thirsty, and dry, calling out for Jesus to change their lives, for Him to fill them with His glory, to come on earth like never before, He is about to sweep through their lives with the power of the Holy Spirit (resurrection power), bringing such life as we have never known. We are truly about

[10] Inside the Chryalis http://learn.tkschools.org/lbaxter/Lists/Announcements/Attachments/8/Inside%20the%20Chrysalis.pdf

to cross over into the promised land, and the promised land is ultimately Jesus Christ as He is the one who promised—He is our inheritance, and we His! He is the Life, and He is about to bring unparalleled life to His hungry and thirsty people. Resurrection power, death to life—a complete cellular change, cocoon to butterfly!

He also spoke these words to me:

> *The old form, the old move of God (caterpillar) has to die so that the new form, the new move of God (butterfly) can come alive! Complete cellular change! Don't be afraid of the old thing dying but rejoice that the new is coming alive!*

Only the Spirit of the Living God can breathe the Breath of Life. The fullness of the Spirit is life! Jesus is the Life!

Because God is about to pour out His Spirit, He is trying to ready His people that we might stand in the midst of Him, pouring out His glory. Malachi says:

> *Suddenly the Lord you are seeking will come to his temple; the messenger of the covenant, whom you desire, will come...But who can endure the day of his coming? Who can stand when he appears? For he will be like a refiner's fire or a launder's soap. He will sit as a refiner and purifier of silver; he will purify the Levites and refine them like gold and silver.* (Malachi 3:1)

He goes on to say that when God does come, He will come near for judgment (to make a decision for or against) and He will be quick to testify against sorcerers, adulterers, perjurers, and those who oppress and deprive of justice but do not have a fear of the Lord.

If God's people are calling out for revival, we need to understand that revival means a return of God's presence to His people in all of His glory and all of His splendour. When God's glory begins to come, there is a refining by fire until all of the dross, and all of the impurities in our lives, are removed, revealing the gold: God's glory! Exodus 24:15–17 reads, "*When Moses went up on the mountain, the cloud covered it, and* <u>*the*</u>

glory of the LORD settled on Mount Sinai. For six days the cloud covered the mountain, and on the seventh day the LORD called to Moses from within the cloud. To the Israelites the glory of the LORD looked like a consuming fire on top of the mountain." Again, we read in Hebrews 12:27–29, *"The words 'once more' indicate the removing of what can be shaken—that is, created things—so that what cannot be shaken may remain. Therefore, since we are receiving a kingdom that cannot be shaken, let us be thankful, and so worship God acceptably with reverence and awe, for our 'God is a consuming fire.'"*

When the glory of God manifests, it looks like a consuming fire, and it first comes and reveals the enemy's activity in our lives, that sin might be stripped away, and His people purified, that we might successfully carry His glory without touching it. When this stripping happens, we must remember and understand that God's glory reveals sin that we might repent of it and have it removed, bringing healing and freedom from the enemy. God, through His glory, brings those things in our lives that *are of Him* to light that they may be seen, and those things in our lives that *are not of God* to light, so they can be removed. Hebrews 4:12–13 says:

> *For the word of God is living and active. Sharper than any double-edged sword, it penetrates even to dividing soul and spirit, joints and marrow; it judges the thoughts and attitudes of the heart. Nothing in all creation is hidden from God's sight. Everything is uncovered and laid bare before the eyes of him to whom we must give account.*

In November 2011, while waiting in a checkout line at the grocery store, I was once again assaulted visually by the barely clothed images of women on all of the magazine covers. The Holy Spirit spoke this brief word to me: *"The enemy is stripping the world of their clothing and revealing their flesh that they might be covered in shame, but I am stripping my people of their flesh that they might be covered in my glory!"*

The enemy is trying to raise up a flood of sexual immorality that will blanket the nations in shame, which is the opposite of God's desire and intent to cover the earth with His glory. *"For the earth will be filled with the knowledge of the glory of the LORD, as the waters cover the sea"* (Habakkuk 2:14). The enemy knows, probably better than we, that when God's glory arises upon God's people and we begin to occupy territory instead of just maintaining, he will be in big trouble because the kingdom of God will advance, covering the earth in glory and relegating him and his cohorts to Hades.

Isaiah 60:1–2 reads, *"Arise, shine, for your light has come, and the glory of the LORD rises upon you. See, darkness covers the earth and thick darkness is over the peoples, but the LORD rises upon you."* My Bible's footnote on this passage says, "When God's people are enabled to live righteous lives through God's power, they are no longer a reproach to his name but *become a light to the world.*"

A CHOSEN VESSEL: FILLED AND COVERED IN GOD'S GLORY?

Pastor John Kilpatrick from Church of His Presence in Mobile, Alabama, brings a wonderful message on the different vessels one finds in the scriptures, and he speaks of the "chosen vessel." He describes the chosen vessel as a piece of clay that the Potter has formed and shaped into a special image. A special piece on which not only will he put his initials, like he does with all other kinds of vessels, but he will write his *full name.* The chosen vessel will bear his *signature.*

The church is God's chosen vessel, to be formed and molded, made into His image, that we might be filled with His glory. Then, bearing His Glorious Name, be poured out into the nations, bringing glory and honour to the Potter whose *signature* we bear. I believe that, as a universal church, we are about to be put back into God's Pottery Kiln. For those who are walking uprightly before their God, and have consistently allowed God's refining fires to work in their lives, the fire of the kiln will feel warm and comforting and will only enhance and strengthen that which God has already worked in them. But for those who have not been walking uprightly, and have been flirting with the world and its fleshly desires, the fire of God's Kiln is going to do one of two things. The fire will either burn off all the dross, because we are willing to humble our hearts and repent as He reveals the areas needing to be refined, or it will harden our hearts of clay, because we are prideful and unwilling to repent. I've heard it said that the same fire that melts wax also hardens clay. The same principle applies when God's glory is poured out upon people. If we have humble hearts and desperately want to follow Jesus and fulfill God's Will and Purposes on earth, then at the presence of God, at the presence of His glory, our hearts will melt like wax and become soft and pliable. But if our hearts are full of sin that we choose to hold onto because of pride, then our hearts will be hardened and turned to clay. This is what happened to Pharaoh in Egypt. God didn't harden his heart. Pharaoh hardened his own heart through pride and a lack of repentance and humility in the face of the presence of the God, for, "*God opposes the proud but gives grace to the humble*" (James 4:6b).

I re-quote what the Holy Spirit spoke to me on Easter Monday: *"God isn't coming to bring judgment on His people; He is coming to bring judgment on the enemy's activity in people's lives. However, if they choose to hold on to their sins (the enemy's activity) then judgment will come upon them, as well."*

In order for us, the people of God, to arise, shine, and have the glory of the LORD rise upon us and in us that we might pour out His presence into a deeply dark world, we must throw off every sin that entangles us, especially sexual immorality. Sexual immorality tramples the Son of God underfoot, allowing the enemy to publicly disgrace our Saviour. As we read in an earlier chapter, *"If we deliberately keep on sinning after we have received the knowledge of the truth, no sacrifice for sins is left (there is no atonement) but only a fearful expectation of judgment and of raging fire that will consume the enemies of God"* (Hebrews 10:26–27). Who are the enemies of God? James 4:4 states, *"You adulterous people, don't you know that friendship with the world is hatred toward God? Anyone who chooses to be a friend of the world becomes an enemy of God."* I don't know about you, but I would much rather be a friend of God than an enemy. I want to be as far away from the line of sin as I can be! I would rather have the Refiner's fire purge me of all sin, that I might be filled with His glory, than to have a fearful expectation of His judgment and raging fire.

Malachi 4:1–6 tells us:

"Surely the day is coming; it will burn like a furnace. All the arrogant and every evildoer will be stubble, and that day that is coming will set them on fire," says the LORD Almighty. "Not a root or a branch will be left to them. But for you who revere my name, the sun of righteousness will rise with healing in its wings...See, I will send you the prophet Elijah before that great and dreadful day of the LORD comes. He will turn the hearts of the fathers (Israel) to their children (Gentiles), and the hearts of the children to their fathers; or else I will come and strike the land with a curse." (Parentheses mine)[11]

As we read again from Romans 11:20b–22:

Do not be arrogant (Gentiles), but be afraid. For if God did not spare the natural branches (Israel), he will not spare you either. Consider therefore the kindness and sternness of God: sternness to those who fell, but kindness to you, provided that you continue in his kindness. Otherwise, you also will be cut off. (Parentheses mine)

So what is God saying? He is saying repent. If you will judge yourself, and throw off every sin that entangles you, especially sexual immorality, then He will not have to judge you. But if He does judge you, humble yourself and He will give you grace. Take the judgment as a father disciplines his son or daughter, and know that He does it for your own good because He loves you. Let your heart become broken and contrite, for a broken and contrite heart He will not turn away.

So how does one throw off every sin that entangles? To be entangled means to be twisted, intertwined, captured, trapped, ensnared, bogged down or mired. A movie called *War Horse* exemplifies this entanglement, and how one can be set free. The movie takes place during World War I, when a young man's beloved horse is shipped off to be a part of the

[11] Many believe this can also mean actual children and fathers.

cavalry. The horse eventually finds himself running frantically from a perceived danger and ends up running into no man's land between the two opposing armies. The no man's land consists of scattered, spiraled barbed wire attached to wooden fence rails. The warhorse runs through the no man's land and quickly becomes entangled in the barbed wire, eventually sinking to the ground, unable to move. In a moment of compassion, a man from one army decides to go out and help the horse free itself. Calling a truce, a man from the other side joins him with some wire cutters. The horse, being so entangled, frightened, tired, and seriously wounded, tries to struggle free from the barbed wire to get away from the men, only to have the barbs dig further into his flesh and the wire tighten around him. Speaking soothingly to the horse, the men finally get him to stay still. One clip at a time, the men snip apart the barbed wire, freeing the horse. Although badly wounded, the horse eventually heals and survives.

So how can this story help you, if you have found yourself so entangled in sexual immorality or any other sin? First, can you picture yourself as the horse, the barbed wire as the sin that has entangled you, and the compassionate men as the Holy Spirit? Then just as the frightened horse became still, knowing it couldn't free itself, and dependent upon the compassionate men to help, call out to the Holy Spirit for help. Acknowledge to Him that you are so entangled in this sin that you can't free yourself and you want Him to come and set you free, and He will. The Holy Spirit will come and begin to snip away, a barb at a time, until you are free. The Holy Spirit will bring conviction, which means to convince, that this sin is something you don't want to be a part of anymore. Don't grit your teeth and try to free yourself. You can't do it. It is a spiritual battle; only the Holy Spirit, as you humble yourself before Him (become dependent on Him), can help you.

> *"'Come now, let us reason together,' says the LORD. 'Though your sins are like scarlet, they shall be as white as snow; though they are red as crimson, they shall be like wool'"* (Isaiah 1:18).
>
> *"Let the wicked forsake his way and the evil man his thoughts. Let him turn to the LORD, and he will have mercy on him, and to our God, for he will freely pardon"* (Isaiah 55:7).

Prayer

Heavenly Father,

I come boldly before your throne of grace to receive help in my time of need. I come with a broken and contrite heart, confessing, repenting, and asking for forgiveness of my sin of ____________, and my sin of trampling on the Son of God, allowing the enemy the right to publicly disgrace my Saviour, Jesus. I acknowledge that despite wanting to be free, I can't do it. I have struggled and struggled to free myself, but have been unable to do so. This sin has entangled me and I can't even move. I cry out to you today, to come and help me. Come with your wire cutters and clip away all of the barbs of this sin from my life that I might be set free. I repent of my sin, and where I don't have full repentance, I ask that you would bring me to an understanding of my sin, so that it can be rooted out of my life. I ask for you, Holy Spirit, to set me free through the power of the blood of Jesus Christ, which He shed on the cross, making atonement for my sin. Cleanse me, Holy Spirit, from all of my unrighteousness and wash me whiter than snow that I might be a chosen vessel, ready to be filled with your glory. I thank you that you love me and I pray for your grace to fill me as I humble myself before you. Help me, by your grace, to make amends where relationships have been hurt and wounded. Help me to be restored in an intimate relationship with you and with those I love. Today, I close the door on the enemy's activity in my life, and I don't grant him access anymore. Fill me now with your Holy Spirit. In Jesus' mighty Name. Amen.

Psalm 24:1–10:

The earth is the LORD's, and everything in it, the world, and all who live in it; for he founded it upon the seas and established it upon the waters.

Who may ascend the hill of the LORD? Who may stand in his holy place?

He who has clean hands and a pure heart, who does not lift up his soul to an idol or swear by what is false.

He will receive blessing from the LORD and vindication from God his saviour.
Such is the generation of those who seek him, who seek your face, O God of Jacob.
Lift up your heads, O you gates; be lifted up, you ancient doors, that the King of glory may come in.
Who is this King of glory? The LORD strong and mighty, the LORD mighty in battle.
Lift up your heads, O you gates; lift them up, you ancient doors, that the King of glory may come in.
Who is he, this King of glory?
The LORD Almighty—he is the King of glory.

In the next chapter, we will address one more question for the Gentile church: how do we become so intimate with Jesus that we will be filled and covered with His glory?

six

THE PRESENCE OF JESUS:
The Indwelling Glory

> *"Therefore come out from them and be separate, says the Lord."*
> (2 Corinthians 6:17)

In Jeremiah 1:10, at the inception of Jeremiah's call as a prophet to Israel, God spoke these words to him: *"See, today I appoint you over the nations and kingdoms to uproot and tear down, to destroy and overthrow, to build and to plant."* Uproot, tear down, destroy, and overthrow are words of judgment. The majority of Jeremiah's prophetic call was the pronouncement of judgment upon Israel. However, we also see that once Jeremiah obeyed and spoke the words of judgment and repentance, he was allowed to proclaim words of restoration, evidenced by the words "to build and to plant." The majority of us would like to skip all of the seemingly negative judgment of uprooting and tearing down and move right to the restoration part, but there is never true restoration without true recognition of sin. We tend to perceive judgment as a terrible thing, when really it is the beginning of restoration. Let's look at the words stated above, and see why they are the beginning of restoring what was lost or never known.

Uproot. Roots, as we know, are not usually visible above ground. We are aware of them, but we don't pay a lot of attention to them unless we're biologists, gardeners, or farmers. Those who do work with vegetation know how important the health of the roots is to the overall plant and crop. My husband and I tried to grow a garden in our backyard a few years ago. For the first couple of years, everything was great and we had a wonderful harvest of vegetables. However, the last two years that we gardened, it rained a lot. The produce started out looking great and flourishing, but suddenly began to rot. Not knowing what was wrong, we asked a biologist friend what was happening to our garden. She came back with the conclusion that it was root rot from too much rain and not enough drainage. The root rot killed the whole plant and harvest. The same principle applies to our lives. If we have good roots, we will have good fruit! Jesus draws near in our lives to inspect our character and behaviour, to see if we are producing healthy fruit. If He notices that the fruit is not flourishing and isn't healthy, then He has to uproot that portion of our lives that *we*, not *He,* might see what is causing the fruit to not produce. This uprooting is not a negative process, if kept in the right perspective. It is a very healthy occurrence in the garden of our character. Bad roots are uprooted only to *reveal* what was once hidden from our eyes, so that changes might be made, producing a healthy harvest. Let us allow Jesus our prophet to uproot (reveal) the enemy's activity in our lives that his activity, once hidden from our spiritual eyes, might be torn down.

Tear down. To tear something down means to dismantle—to take to pieces. Dismantle comes from an old French term *des* (expressing reversal) and the Latin *mantler,* meaning to fortify (strengthen). Satan is the father of lies and he sows deception into our hearts, minds, and spirit. However, our prophet Jesus comes and begins to dismantle Satan's lies. Jesus helps us to see that what we used to think was true was really a lie. He comes and convinces us of the truth so the enemy's activity will be dismantled, and everything the enemy was trying to build up and make strong in our lives is reversed—destroyed—and replaced with His truth.

Destroyed. To destroy something suggests a removal from existence, a complete ruin, and again, expresses reversal. Jesus reveals the enemy's hidden activity by uprooting it, then He tears to pieces the enemy's lies that were once erect and strong, ruining the enemy's strongholds, removing them from existence in our lives. Thus, Jesus overthrows the secret work of the enemy and sin in our lives.

Overthrow. To overthrow something means to remove forcibly from power and put an end to it. Our prophet Jesus comes with His word like a hammer and a fire, forcibly removing the enemy's activity from having power over our lives. We then can close the door in that area of our lives, as the enemy has been overthrown![12]

Let us not perceive Jesus' drawing near to judge, to make a decision for or against, as a negative thing. Let us recognize that His judging and refining fire comes to reveal, uproot, and dismantle the enemy's activity, weakening the enemy in our lives. He destroys the enemy's work from existence, bringing about a complete reversal of his activity, forcibly removing and overthrowing the enemy, putting an end to his activity, and closing the door in his face that he would no longer have access. This leaves Jesus full entrance to fill our lives.

Have you ever observed this process in your life? I certainly have, but I didn't always understand how or why certain things were happening in the order they were taking place. For example, a while ago, God brought a revelation to me of my "adoption" into the family of God. I had understood God's unconditional love for many years; however, there still seemed to be a puzzle piece missing in my understanding of the gospel. This left me, at times, feeling insecure and rejected. As the revelation of the spirit of adoption came, I began to understand and feel more secure, and yet there were still trying moments when I felt rejected. This first step of revelation was God *uprooting and revealing* the enemy's activity, which was working through a spirit of rejection. In the next few months, God began to *dismantle and tear down* the enemy's activity surrounding rejection. He tore it to pieces and convinced me of the lies of the enemy. Then He began to destroy the stronghold of rejection in my life, through teaching me more about my adoption, inheritance, and authority as a daughter of God, an heir and co-heir with Christ.

---

[12] *New Oxford American Dictionary, Second Edition*, Erin McKean (editor), May 2005, Oxford University Press.

A few months later, after God guided me biblically through the revelation of adoption, He awoke me one morning with these words: *"Rachel, reject the spirit of rejection, and welcome the spirit of adoption."* When I got up and went into prayer, that is exactly what I did. This was the final overthrowing of the enemy. With the power and authority I now knew I had over the enemy because of my adoption, and a full revelation of this truth, I was able to forcibly remove the enemy from having any power to make me feel rejected. He could no longer operate in my life through rejection, because his lies and activity had been uprooted, torn down, destroyed, and overthrown! Hallelujah, praise Jesus! We can all expect this to transpire in every area that the Holy Spirit identifies.

Jesus then speaks words of *restoration, building,* and *planting*. He comes and plants healthy roots, producing spiritual fruit that won't rot but will flourish and nourish those who partake of it from our lives. He also builds, erecting a strong, fortified temple in our lives that cannot be destroyed or overthrown by the enemy, but can house Jesus' presence—the presence of the living God in all of His glory and splendour.

The first four chapters covered Jesus approaching and speaking words of uprooting, tearing down, destroying, and overthrowing the enemy's activity of sexual immorality in the life of His church. This is so He can speak restoration, building, and planting. Judgment removes all that is not of Jesus, and restoration prepares a resting place for His Spirit to dwell. Jeremiah states in 31:28, *"'Just as I watched over them to uproot and tear down, and to overthrow, destroy and bring disaster, so I will watch over them to build and to plant,' declares the LORD."*

God promised that He would dwell with us and walk among us. Therefore, we are to separate our "temples" from participating in that which the world participates, that we might be acceptable dwelling places for the presence of Jesus. We are to perfect holiness, without which no one will see God.

> *What agreement is there between the temple of God and idols? For we are the temple of the living God. As God has said: "I will live with them and walk among them, and I will be their God, and they*

> *will be my people." Therefore come out from them and be separate, says the Lord. Touch no unclean thing, and I will receive you. I will be a Father to you and you will be my sons and daughters, says the Lord Almighty.*
> *Since we have these promises, dear friends, let us purify ourselves from everything that contaminates body and spirit, perfecting holiness out of reverence for God.* (2 Corinthians 6:16–7:1)

It is an extreme mystery to me that God chose lowly humans to carry His presence. Before God created the foundations of the earth, He chose us as vessels, as adopted sons and daughters, to be the resting and dwelling place of God. Jesus, having obeyed the Father even unto death, sat down at His right hand and received the promised Holy Spirit that He might pour Him into all mankind. Jesus poured out the gift of the abundant, holy life of the Trinity into every person willing to humble his or her heart and repent.

At the point of our salvation, a deposit of the Holy Spirit was given to each of us. The Bible teaches that through the grace and empowerment of the Holy Spirit, we are to work out our salvation in fear and trembling, for our God is a consuming fire. The living God who is on one hand so unconditionally loving that He would send His only begotten Son, Jesus, to be sacrificed as atonement for our sins that we might be adopted, is also a God to be revered and feared, as He is so holy.

Contemplating who the living God is, and the idea that we are to house His glory, causes me to tremble at the thought that we are going to be so full of His presence that the whole earth will be covered with His glory! Reading the biblical accounts of the times God allowed His glory to be poured out with nothing hidden or held back causes me to prepare my heart for what I am truly asking when I say, "Fill me with your glory, Lord!" Moses had to be hidden behind a rock to handle catching a mere glimpse of God's presence. Priests could only enter the Holy of Holies once a year to make atonement on behalf of the people, and everything had to be in divine order to do so. Uzzah was struck dead for reaching out to steady the Ark of the Covenant, which at that time housed God's presence.

You might be thinking, "Yes, but now we have Jesus, who is the rock behind which we are hidden, and we are covered by His shed blood unlike the priests, and now we can enter boldly into God's presence." True. However, the story of Ananias and Sapphira in Acts sits squarely within these New Testament parameters, but because they both decided beforehand to lie to the apostles, they both died. God's glory was so present in the apostles that sin was judged instantly. (Acts 5:1–11)

I believe it wise to understand whom we are seeking when we seek to house God's glory. I don't believe one is to carelessly handle the glory of God because we are under grace. However, recognizing God's holiness is not to be a deterrent from drawing near to God, as there is far more protection in His presence than without. Let me explain why I suggest understanding the God whose presence and glory we seek.

Seven years ago, I had a profound encounter with God, from which His power and His presence began to manifest quite strongly. During this time, God gave me a prophetic directive for our church, and when I shared it with my pastor and his wife, the office filled with His tangible, weighty presence. His presence was glorious and beautiful. Shortly after, because I was missing the revelation of the spirit of adoption mentioned earlier in this chapter, I became afraid of God's power and pulled back from obeying the prophetic word, and from His presence. God's glory withdrew, and He heavily convicted me a few months later for not obeying Him. Although I still walked in a relationship with Jesus, as He had forgiven me, I could no longer feel or sense the awesome presence of God quite as I had previously. It took years, and a lot of wrestling, testing, and refining with God, before He allowed me to once again begin to be filled with His glory. Carrying His presence is a precious honour, which I do not take lightly. Throughout this process, I found two things missing in my understanding: (1) I didn't understand the importance of God speaking a prophetic word, and obeying the directive, and (2) I didn't have a full revelation of my adoption, which made me fearful of His power.

What I am about to share with you is a pattern the Lord showed me, a template for a house with a strong foundation for housing His glory. If the revelations of this template are in place, it gives us protection from touching God's glory, as He will not give His glory to another, and it gives reassurance of our rightful place in Him as a son or daughter that we need not fear His power. A quote from John Bevere says, "The 'fear of God' draws us to Him and the 'love of God' reassures you as you come."

Although it would be desirable to share this template in extensive detail, it is outside the scope of this book as it could easily encompass a whole other book. Therefore, I will list the template and show it as a house template with a corresponding scripture to give you an indication of the idea. I have laid out the fundamental elements, which will allow you to receive the pattern in hopes of starting your own journey of personal revelation in the areas required.

Please note: as I reference the term revelation, I am referring to the Holy Spirit's work of illuminating previous revealed truths—as written in scripture—as a fresh impartation upon your heart. Therefore, it moves from just a teaching or factual knowledge to a revelation—an unveiling of a divine truth, allowing one to fully comprehend God's Word.

GOD'S SPIRITUAL HOUSE TEMPLATE:
SUSTAINING HIS GLORY

Foundation

Revelations of:

1) The Cornerstone: Salvation through Jesus Christ, the Son of God
2) The Spirit of Adoption
3) Humility
4) Fear of the Lord

Lead to:

House Walls

5) Speaking truth in love
6) Unity

Filling us with:

7) Peace
8) Sabbath Rest/Promised Land

Revelations of…

Foundation

1) Cornerstone: Jesus, the firm foundation on which the whole house is built.

"So this is what the Sovereign LORD says: 'See, I lay a stone in Zion, a tested stone, a precious cornerstone for a sure foundation; the one who trusts will never be dismayed.'" (Isaiah 28:16)

a) Salvation: Revelation that Jesus is the Son of the Living God bringing godly repentance and not worldly sorrow. *"Godly sorrow brings repentance that leads to salvation and leaves no regret, but worldly sorrow brings death"* (2 Corinthians 7:10).

These next three revelations must be in place for the spirit of Jesus to be real to you, and for the glory of God to dwell in you in all of His fullness and splendour! One will not touch His glory when these foundational revelations are securely in place. Please note that I have said a revelation and not just a teaching.

2) Spirit of Adoption: *"For he chose us in him before the creation of the world to be holy and blameless in his sight. In love he predestined us to be adopted as his sons through Jesus Christ, in accordance with his pleasure and will…"* (Ephesians 1:4–5)
3) Humility: Jesus, *"…Who, being in very nature God, did not consider equality with God…but made himself nothing, taking the very nature of a servant, being made in human likeness"* (Philippians 2:6–7).
4) Fear of the Lord: *"Then I saw another angel flying in midair, and he had the eternal gospel to proclaim to those who live on the earth—to every nation, tribe, language and people. He said in a loud voice, 'Fear God and give him glory, because the hour of his judgment has come. Worship him who made the heavens, the earth, the sea and the springs of water"* (Revelation 14:6–7).

Lead to…

House Walls: When the above foundational revelations are in place, one can speak truth in love to self, hear truth in love from God, and can speak truth in love to others, bringing wholeness and life—even if it is pinpointing a weakness or a sin.

5) Speak truth in love:

> *Instead, speaking the truth in love, we will in all things grow up into him who is the Head, that is, Christ. From him the whole body, joined and held together by every supporting ligament, grows and builds itself up in love, as each part does its work.* (Ephesians 4:15–16)

When we are speaking truth in love, undergirded by the foundational revelations of adoption, humility, and reverence for God, it brings oneness of mind, heart, and purpose within self, between self and God, between one another, and corporately within community churches and the universal body of Christ. Unity then brings peace and the commanded blessings of God, and with ever-increasing glory we give Jesus a place to rest and dwell with His people. We enter our Sabbath Rest and our Christian lives exhibit, not by might, nor by power but by His Spirit (Zechariah 4:6).

6) Unity:

> *Be completely humble and gentle; be patient, bearing with one another in love. Make every effort to keep the unity of the Spirit through the bond of peace. There is one body and one Spirit—just as you were called to one hope when you were called—one Lord, one faith, one baptism; one God and Father of all, who is over all and through all and in all.* (Ephesians 4:2–6)

House Filled With…
7) Peace:

Finally, brothers, rejoice. Aim for restoration, comfort one another, agree with one another, live in peace; and the God of love and peace will be with you (2 Corinthians 13:11, ESV).

8) Sabbath Rest/Promised Land:

There remains, then, a Sabbath-rest for the people of God; for anyone who enters God's rest also rests from his own work, just as God did from his. Let us, therefore, make every effort to enter that rest… (Hebrews 4:9–10)

Prayer

Abba, Father, pour out your spirit upon your son/daughter. Bring them revelation of their adoption into your family. Let them receive the unveiling of their inheritance as an heir of God and co-heir of Christ. Bring understanding of their connection within the life of the Trinity—the Father, the Son, and the Holy Spirit. Let their spirit receive your love being shed abroad in their hearts through the Holy Spirit. May they move into a deep humility and dependence upon their God, just like their older brother, Jesus. Let a spirit of the Fear of the Lord come upon them, bringing a firm foundation to house your glory. Abba, fill them with the Truth, that they might speak your truth in love to themselves, and to one another. Let unity and oneness of mind, heart, and purpose overtake their relationships with family, friends, and fellow Christians, filling them with your peace that surpasses all understanding. Peace that has nothing missing and nothing broken. Peace that leads them into their Sabbath of resting in your presence and bringing their spiritual home to completion, that you might not just visit, but dwell and inhabit your child's life! In Jesus' Name. Amen.

CONCLUSION

The Gentile church, as adopted, covenant children of God, have a tremendous mandate to cast off all fleshly desires—especially sexual immorality, which leaves us desolate of God's presence, and compromises our children and future generations—entering into a deep, intimate relationship with Jesus Christ, that we might be filled with His glory and splendour. Being so in-dwelt by the glory of God, we can then release a corporate prophetic voice to the nations, awakening their conscience to sin that they might repent, turn, and be saved. Let us work diligently, as the apostle Paul did, to bring in the fullness of the Gentiles to salvation. In so doing, that we might in turn, by the glory of God dwelling in us, bring Israel to envy that they may receive a revelation of their Messiah, and be saved! *Let us become like an Esther, so intimate with our heavenly king that we would find favour and effectively intercede on behalf of the Jewish nation!*

DANIEL'S PRAYER FOR HIS PEOPLE

I will leave you with a portion of Daniel's prayer from the book of Daniel, Chapter 9. Daniel is in exile with his countrymen and has been studying the scriptures of the prophet Jeremiah concerning God's judgment on the nation. Realizing that the desolation of Jerusalem was to last seventy years, Daniel understands that God is revealing this to him as an invitation to intercede on Israel's behalf so that the promise of Israel's restoration to their land might be fulfilled on God's appointed timetable. Daniel's prayer establishes a precedence of confessing then repenting for sins and interceding before God for mercy and forgiveness. His prayer identifies a personal confession as well as a corporate identification with the sins of the nations. Although Daniel was not involved in the sins he was confessing before God, he identified with the community of Israel as if the sins were his own. Thus, he was able to effectively intercede on their behalf.

As you read Daniel's prayer, meditate on its significance as an analogy to one's own temple. Meditate on and question—as individual and corporate Christians—whether we have listened to God's commands and laws concerning sexual immorality. Remember, He says, "not even a hint" is proper in God's house. Have we listened to God's prophets (preachers) who speak with His authority? Do we truly believe that God is right and we are wrong? Do we believe we cover ourselves, our children, and future generations with shame when we scorn His commands? Do we believe we have disobeyed His instructions and refused to listen to His voice? Do we believe that the desolation within our bodily temples is desolate of God's glory and presence because we have engaged in some form of sexual immorality? Do we believe God is a covenant-keeping God whether we choose life or death, blessing or curses? Do we refuse to seek mercy from the Lord our God by turning from our sins and recognizing His truth? Do we believe the secular world around us, Gentile and Jewish alike, mock us because we participate in the sins of the world just as they do?

If you do believe, consider repenting like Daniel on behalf of self and intercede for the corporate body that we might receive mercy and forgiveness from a great and awesome God who is righteous and full of love to those who obey His commands. Request that He hear us as we repent and confess our sins of sexual immorality that has caused a desolation of His presence. Ask Him to look upon us again because of His righteousness, not ours. Cry out to God for His mercy, forgiveness, and grace to overtake His people once again that we might fulfill His mandate of having our temples filled with His glory that we might bear His signature, bringing in the harvest of Gentiles, effectively pleading for the salvation of Jerusalem, His holy mountain, one more time!

> *So I turned to the Lord God and pleaded with him in prayer and petition, in fasting, and in sackcloth and ashes. I prayed to the Lord my God and confessed:*
> *"Lord, the great and awesome God, who keeps his covenant of love with those who love him and keep his commandments, we have sinned and done wrong. We have been wicked and have rebelled; we have turned away from your commands and laws. We have not listened to your servants the prophets, who spoke in your name to our kings, our princes and our ancestors, and to all the people of the land.*
> *"Lord, you are righteous, but this day we are covered with shame—the people of Judah and the inhabitants of Jerusalem and all Israel, both near and far, in all the countries where you have scattered us because of our unfaithfulness to you. We and our kings, our princes and our ancestors are covered with shame, Lord, because we have sinned against you. The Lord our God is merciful and forgiving, even though we have rebelled against him; we have not obeyed the Lord our God or kept the laws he gave us through his servants the prophets. All Israel has transgressed your law and turned away, refusing to obey you.*
> *"Therefore the curses and sworn judgments written in the Law of Moses, the servant of God, have been poured out on us, because we have sinned against you. You have fulfilled the words spoken against us and against our rulers by bringing on us great disaster. Under the whole heaven nothing has ever been done like what has been done to Jerusalem. Just as it is written in the Law of Moses, all this disaster has come on us, yet we have not sought the favor of the Lord our God by turning from our sins and giving attention to your truth. The Lord did not hesitate to bring the disaster on us, for the Lord our God is righteous in everything he does; yet we have not obeyed him.*

"Now, Lord our God, who brought your people out of Egypt with a mighty hand and who made for yourself a name that endures to this day, we have sinned, we have done wrong. Lord, in keeping with all your righteous acts, turn away your anger and your wrath from Jerusalem, your city, your holy hill. Our sins and the iniquities of our ancestors have made Jerusalem and your people an object of scorn to all those around us.

"Now, our God, hear the prayers and petitions of your servant. For your sake, Lord, look with favor on your desolate sanctuary. Give ear, our God, and hear; open your eyes and see the desolation of the city that bears your Name. We do not make requests of you because we are righteous, but because of your great mercy. Lord, listen! Lord, forgive! Lord, hear and act! For your sake, my God, do not delay, because your city and your people bear your Name."

...I was speaking and praying, confessing my sin and the sin of my people Israel and making my request to the Lord my God for his holy hill... (Daniel 9:3–20)

CPSIA information can be obtained at www.ICGtesting.com
Printed in the USA
LVOW082123260413

331163LV00002B/45/P

9 781770 697928